Down to Earth

Down to Earth

A Fighter Pilot's Experiences of
Surviving Dunkirk, the Battle
of Britain, Dieppe and D-Day

Squadron Leader K.B. McGlashan AFC

with

Owen Zupp

GRUB STREET · LONDON

Published by
Grub Street
4 Rainham Close
London
SW11 6SS

First published 2007

British Library Cataloguing in Publication Data
McGlashan, Kenneth Butterworth
  Down to earth
  1. McGlashan, Kenneth Butterworth 2. Great Britain. Royal
  Air Force – History – World War, 1939-1945 3. Fighter
  Pilots – Great Britain – Biography 4. World War, 1939-1945
  – Personal narratives, British 5. World War, 1939-1945 –
  Aerial operations, British
  I. Title II. Zupp, Owen
  940.5'44941'092

ISBN-13: 9781904943846

Cover design by Lizzie B design

Typeset by Pearl Graphics, Hemel Hempstead

Printed and bound by MPG Ltd, Bodmin, Cornwall

Grub Street only uses
FSC (Forest Stewardship Council) paper for its books.

Dedication
For Doreen. My beloved wife and best friend for our
wonderful life together over these sixty-three years.

Our thanks to:
John and Laura Ethel McGlashan; 'Ma' Wilson; our five beautiful
daughters; Owen Zupp; Chris McGrath; Jill Freestone; Dr Toby
& Mrs Joane de Milt Severne; Group Captain & Mrs Trevor Bryant-Fenn;
all of the landlords and landladies of the UK who welcomed us into
their homes; and all of our friends and colleagues who served
in that great institution the Royal Air Force.
Kenneth and Doreen McGlashan

Contents

Acknowledgements

In the course of researching and writing *Down to Earth*, it was my privilege to meet and correspond with a vast array of wonderful people. Without their many and varied contributions, the fascinating tale of Squadron Leader Kenneth McGlashan AFC and Hawker Hurricane R-DX may never have been recorded.

Most importantly, my thanks to Kenneth and Doreen McGlashan and their family for welcoming me into their home and sharing their amazing journey with me. Thanks also to Chris McGrath for introducing me to this tremendous couple.

To Kenneth's former navigator, Ken Lusty, a gratitude of thanks for an external perspective of the man at work through the D-Day landings. Tracking Ken down would not have been possible without the enthusiastic assistance of Ed McManus of the Battle of Britain Historical Society. Also, to the numerous RAF squadron associations that thumbed through their archives for any trace of Kenneth's service with their unit, my thanks.

Rick Roberts is the man who is dedicated to seeing Kenneth's recovered Hawker Hurricane R-DX return to its former glory and once again take to the sky. For generously introducing me to this airframe as it grew from the ground up and extending the hospitality of his home on my visits to the UK, I am truly indebted.

Thank you to my brother Adrian, for his literary mentorship. Finally, to my wife Kirrily and my daughters Ruby, Hannah and Elizabeth. My unending gratitude for your patience through the very early mornings and the equally late nights that were needed to make this book a reality.

Owen Zupp

CHAPTER ONE

Dunkirk

The English Channel spans only twenty-one miles at its narrowest point, yet this small passage of water has carried the legions of the Roman Empire, borne witness to the Norman Conquests and hosted clashes with the Spanish Armada. On the final day of spring in 1940, as a raw nineteen-year-old Royal Air Force pilot, I was perched at 25,000 feet witnessing another chapter in the Channel's long history.

The French First Army, the Belgian Army and the British Expeditionary Force were encircled on the coast of Northern France by the advancing German forces. As Panzers bore down on what remained of allied defensive positions, the rest fell back to the shoreline. The Battle of France was lost and Operation Dynamo was seeking to evacuate the troops across the Channel using all and sundry vessels to access the shallows of the coastline near Dunkirk. To the east, the pall of smoke from burning oil and the haze of devastation hung over the evacuation. The narrow Channel was now all that separated Britain from the same fate that had overrun Europe.

My view of history was through the glasshouse-like canopy of my Hawker Hurricane Mk I serial number P2902, and wearing the broad markings, 'R-DX' along her camouflaged flanks. Whilst 'DX' was the code allocated to 245 Squadron, 'R for Robert' identified the individual machine. Fresh from the factory with only eight flight hours in her logs, my single-engined fighter cut through the sky at over 300 mph and was armed with eight Browning .303s. It had the reassuring benefit of armour plating behind the pilot's seat and self-sealing petrol tanks that its predecessors had lacked. Nevertheless, we still waged war with the primitive TR9D radio. Selecting a frequency could be likened to finding a modern-day television channel through a sea of white hash and interference. Of course, in the midst of combat, a pilot had limited free hands to attend to such a job. For the moment, my hands were solely occupied by the task of maintaining formation and steering a course for Dunkirk.

Our base at Hawkinge sat a stone's throw from the white cliffs of Dover and we had departed that morning destined for the nearby French coast. I was leading the rear section, whose role was to fly as protective cover for the three flights ahead. 'Watching their backs' as it were, whilst they sought out and attacked the enemy bombers that were intent on pounding our lads. We were a section of three, flying in a tight V, or 'Vic', formation. Behind and to my left was Sergeant Alan Hedges, while Sergeant Geoff Howitt mirrored his position to my right. With the exception of the plume rising up from Dunkirk, the sky was crisp and clear with tremendous visibility. Midway across the Channel, Hedges reported fluctuating oil pressure and, unable to rectify the problem, peeled off towards England. This left Howitt and I to continue as a pair, locked together with the invisible glue that constituted tight formation. As Dunkirk approached beneath my Hurricane's nose, a group of German bombers were spotted lower down and approaching the township. Determined to create even more havoc for the demoralised troops, the Dorniers, Heinkels and Junkers 87s had relentlessly pounded the site of the evacuation for days. Our leading three flights were quick to their task and dived down to engage the bombers with Howitt and me in tow.

As the battle developed beneath me, two fighters, Messerschmitt Bf109s, slipped by 3,000 feet below emerging ahead and to my right at a great rate of knots. They were obviously seeking out the tails of my leading sections and had positioned themselves in the classic six o'clock position. I flicked my gun switch to 'fire' and readied to roll my machine over to initiate a diving attack on the fighters. A screech came over my ineffectual TR9D radio, filling my helmet with deafening, squawking static. I later learned it was Geoff Howitt warning me of the five 109s diving on us, attacking from our port quarter. Howitt broke hard left and crossed in front of me, yet I was still none the wiser. Amidst this melee, I was concentrating on my attack and had totally neglected to look behind. The first indication I had of anything being wrong was when the armour plate behind my head began ringing like an alarm clock. Before I could draw breath, bright red tracers started bombarding my cockpit, whistling between my legs and ravaging the panels of Perspex and fabric to my left. The incendiary-tipped tracers assist the pilot in seeing where his shots are landing and from my perspective I could see them landing very well. As my instrument panel began disintegrating before my eyes, my thoughts leapt suddenly to the vapour-rich petrol tank that sat just behind the instruments. Momentary horror turned to quick relief when I recalled that the tank was self-sealing.

The attack had been lightning fast. I slammed the control stick forward and to the right, entering a downward roll and sending the world spinning around. The back of my legs stung as metal splinters spat from the maze of piping fragmenting beneath my feet. Engine coolant, oil and all variety of hot fluids showered me as the scent of smoke began to fill the air. Foolishly I had been flying with my goggles atop my helmet and now the mix of smoke and oils that were bringing down my aeroplane were also partially blinding me. My cockpit had become a scene of absolute chaos. Then, as quickly as it had begun, the attack abated. Gathering my thoughts, I pulled the aircraft out of the dive and assessed my situation; not good. Bleeding oil and coolant, I knew my Hurricane was done for and I began readying myself to bail out. With the threat of fire growing, I cut the engine, switched off the fuel and set about sliding back the hood. My vision was getting worse and I fumbled to get the canopy back. Three times I tried and three times it slid closed. In my enthusiasm to get out, I was failing to lock the canopy open and a sense of incarceration came across me. Being trapped in a fiery cockpit was the dread of every fighter pilot and for a moment I began to wonder if this was how my war was to end. A moment after that, the second attack started.

The left-hand side of my canopy exploded again as the red tracer ravaged what remained of my aircraft's port side. With the engine shutdown, I was literally powerless. Again I slammed the stick forward, though this time to the left. I combined inertia with gravity, accelerating my wounded machine downwards. I felt a wallop and then a trickling sensation down the back of my leg and I thought that I'd copped a hit in the backside (it turned out to be a direct hit on an Agfa cartridge in my pocket, allowing the film to unfurl in my trousers). Headlong, vertical and hurtling towards terra firma, I had a moment of unexpected clarity and recalled banter at the bar that formed a consensus that 109s were poor at recovering from dives. With the earth looming large in the windscreen and absolutely nothing left to lose, I decided to test this theory. At the last possible moment I hauled back on the control column with all of my remaining might. As the blood drained from my head, my world faded to black and white and then just black.

When I came to, I was beetling along in level flight at the grand altitude of ten feet towards Dunkirk. I weaved myself a path between the sea of abandoned trucks, lorries and equipment that covered the beach. It was a surreal scene. With the water lapping at half tide, I chose a place parallel to the shore to put down my battered, and now decelerating, fighter. The shards of glass and metal that had been flung about the cockpit had sliced through my gloves, so it was with tentative fingertips that I reached down to the greasy gun-firing switch to make it safe before landing. In the process, I bumped the firing button and unleashed a short burst from my Brownings down the beach. Slower, ever slower, I eased the Hurricane on to the sand in a passage between two of the countless abandoned vehicles. Sliding to a halt, the radiator beneath my aircraft dug in to the sand, heaving the Hurricane up on to its nose. As images of flipping over and having to extricate myself from a sand-locked, inverted cockpit flashed before me, the aircraft teetered and fell back onto its belly.

Even now, I was not convinced that I'd shaken my Messerschmitt loose and half expected him to finish the job he'd started. I flung the shattered canopy back, unstrapped, threw my helmet and oxygen mask over the side and leapt out of the cockpit. Looking around desperately, I took cover beneath an abandoned truck where I hoped to gather my thoughts and work out my next move. Suddenly, something grabbed my ankle. Looking down I saw it was a large black hand. It dragged me from my shelter and two French colonial troops lifted me to my feet and backed me up against the truck. Whilst they appeared to be Algerian, my attention was more focused on the long razor sharp bayonets they had pressed deep in to my Mae West life jacket. They began asking in French whether I was German, to which I fervently replied, "Non! Non! Anglais!" I ventured into my best schoolboy

French: "Je suis Anglais". Still no relief. As they gnashed their teeth and pierced me with their crazy eyes, I couldn't help wondering if my short, unintentional burst of gunfire down the beach had played a part in this unfolding drama. They seemed to be discussing whether to finish me off, there and then. Things were getting to fever pitch when I spotted two armed British soldiers, 'Green Howards' I think, walking along the beach. I called out to them with all the strength I could muster and they, in turn, came to my aid. Much to my relief, they set the Algerians to flight and for the second time that day I had a very fortunate escape.

The rescuing 'Tommys' were from a bren gun section positioned a short distance away awaiting the arrival of German Panzers. They had the unenviable task of staring down German armour with what was tantamount to a pea-shooter. To compound their situation, they were low on ammunition. They eyed my forlorn Hurricane and asked if I had any .303 ammunition left. "Lots", I replied as we made our way to R-DX. I opened the gun compartments in the wings to reveal the intertwining belts of ammunition. "It's DeWilde", I explained, knowing that Geneva Convention did not permit the combination of incendiary, armour piercing and explosive bullets for use against personnel. This didn't deter them and they loaded up with as much ammunition as they could carry. With belts of .303 draped across their shoulders they vanished in the direction of their outpost to keep their appointment with the Hun. I have since wondered what fate befell those lads, though in my heart there is no real mystery.

Alone again, I decided that I should destroy my aircraft, particularly as it carried the highly secret 'identification friend or foe' (IFF) unit. Located aft of the pilot's seat, this small box served to signal British ground-based radar of the aircraft status as 'friendly'. Standing on the wing, I took an oil-soaked map from my pocket and attempted to light it before throwing it into the cockpit. As my luck was running, I couldn't light the map. It was probably soaked in relatively flame resistant glycol rather than the other many flammable fluids that were sloshing around my cockpit. I was still attempting to light the map when a loud CRACK and a WHIZZ straightened me up. They were sounds I recognised from my schooldays when I had spent many hours manning the butts and marking targets at the rifle range. Unfortunately, today I was the target for some German infantrymen. I hauled my parachute from the cockpit, threw it over my back, subconsciously thinking it would protect my backside, and made best speed up the beach towards the smoking township of Dunkirk.

As the shooting stopped, I relaxed my pace to a walk and estimated the township lay about nine miles ahead. It was evidently still the focus of the bombardment, as were the ships waiting to evacuate troops. It was an eerie sensation walking along the beach surrounded by the debris of battle, whilst a fierce air battle continued to rage overhead. I can honestly say that I have never felt more alone than when I traipsed along that beach, a nineteen year old on a foreign shore in the midst of war. The rattling of machine-gun fire and the pounding from an anti-aircraft battery filled the air. With expended cartridges and ammo belt links returning to earth, metal seemed to be falling out of the sky all around me so I stopped to pick up a discarded tin hat. Shortly thereafter, I stumbled upon a Colt .45 automatic pistol embossed with the RAF insignia. 'Kitted up', I continued to trudge towards Dunkirk and witnessed a Spitfire plunge into the sea before me and then another lose his clash with the enemy and meet the same watery fate.

Finally I made it to the bottom of the Eastern mole where the wooden breakwater was serving as the point of dispatch for the thousands of troops evacuating the beach. It had obviously been the object of recent battery as it had been holed in a number of places and subsequently patched with makeshift planking. My aerial combat had occurred nearby and it was quite likely that the bombers we had sought were responsible for the damage. The army clearing post was working at capacity as the medical processing centre 'triaged' the wounded and dying. To one side stood a lone Tommy, overseeing a group of German prisoners as they dug a mass grave. There was still sporadic shelling taking place and I took the lead of some soldiers who moved into the fresh craters once things had settled down. Their belief obviously being based on the theory that lightning never strikes twice.

I sat and gathered my breath and thoughts. The scene around me was one of despondency as dejected troops sat in their muddy holes with their eyes downcast. In contrast, I spotted a very upright naval captain coming off the mole. Cane in hand and gas mask slung from his shoulder, as per regulations, he was picking his way through the mess with a genuine air of authority. I righted myself, still holding my parachute, approached the captain and asked, "Sir. How could I return to England?" Without hesitation he instructed me to walk out on the mole where I would find a paddle steamer, *The Golden Eagle*, moored on the left-hand side. He turned away, continued on and I made my way onto the mole. The walk seemed to go on for miles, exacerbated as I was by my surroundings. Stepping over planks on the holed parts, I surveyed the floating sea of humanity that filled the water. Dead soldiery, and pieces thereof, were bobbing up and down with the water's endless motion.

As promised, moored to port, sat an old single-stacked paddle steamer. I boarded her and made my way straight to the first aid post. Here my eyes were rinsed clear of the various fluids that had sprayed around my cockpit and I sought attention for the splinters in my legs. Many of these fragments were to make their way to the surface in the ensuing weeks, whilst others were to remain with me for life. Stationary and full of troops, *The Golden Eagle* was an obvious target for the German bombers. Waiting to cast off was a very nervous period as the area was still extremely active. Finally, much to my relief, we got underway and set out to sea through the maze of anchored shipping. Entering relatively clear water, safety was still not at hand as a Dornier took an interest in us and lined up for a bombing run. He made two attacks and missed us on both attempts. I believe this was due to the captain's tremendous ability to make the vessel twitch and dance out of the way as the Hun ended his bombing run by alternating the paddles either side at full speed, thence into reverse. However, the Dornier persisted and turned in for a third attempt at us. Nearby, a destroyer that had been firing at another enemy aircraft turned its attention to our Dornier. The bomber closed in as the destroyer's guns tracked the closing foe and I waited for one or the other to deliver a fatal blow. Fortunately, the ship's guns were the first to erupt and hurl their shells skyward. The glasshouse nose of the German bomber exploded in front of me as the projectile struck home with devastating effect. Once threatening, the shattered bomber crashed into the sea to the accompaniment of our cheers aboard *The Golden Eagle*.

Things then settled down and we ploughed our way back to English shores, yet there was still one twist of fate to take place. As I sat below decks reflecting on the events of the day, another air battle raged overhead. One of our Hurricanes was locked in combat with a twin-engined Messerschmitt Me110; combat which saw both aircraft destroyed and a lone parachute drift to earth. Noting the winding down of the engines I returned upstairs to see what was the cause of the latest obstacle to my return home. It was a pilot, swimming with all his might in the direction of England. Again with deft skill, the captain jockeyed his vessel towards the aquatic aviator and brought the paddles to a halt so that they may serve as a ladder of sorts. Much to my surprise, as the sodden pilot climbed aboard, I recognised him at once. It was Vic Verity, a New Zealander and fellow pupil from my days of training at Hullavington. Only six months had passed since then, but as we made our way home to England it seemed a world away.

CHAPTER TWO

Into the Blue

My first memory of any consequence was carrying a large, feral black cat, hooked over one arm, into the rear of our three-storey terrace in Bearsden, Dunbartonshire, Scotland. Though only four, or five, years of age at the time, I can still recall my mother's horrified reception. I think she got rid of the cat.

My father was abroad, growing and processing sugar in the Central Provinces of India, utilising local labour. The project had its origins before World War One and was originally conducted with the blessing of the Indian Government. However, government support for the scheme disappeared with the outbreak of war, leaving my father out of pocket and compelled to personally repay those who had invested in the scheme. Presumably because of these factors we left our home and a house named 'Clachaig' at 40 Drymen Road, Bearsden became our residence.

Along with two older sisters and two older brothers, we lived in Bearsden with our Gordon Setter, Gyp. An accomplished thief, Gyp would take himself for a morning constitutional each day and return to our doorstep with a hot breakfast roll. My infant schooling took place in the public hall with about twenty other children. From there it was to Bearsden Academy for my primary education, and subsequently to the Glasgow Academy, a well known institution enjoying public school status.

It was to this backdrop that I had my first taste of flying when an Australian group was offering 'joy flights' at nearby Abbotsinch Airport in Glasgow. At five shillings per ride the cost was not insignificant. Even so, I found myself strapped into the front cockpit of a de Havilland Gipsy Moth biplane. Complete with leather helmet and goggles, I watched in amazement as the earth dropped away. Perched behind the spinning disc, the slipstream rushed past as we climbed for altitude. Wheeling around the sky, the pilot proceeded to demonstrate a series of loops and rolls. I was absolutely enchanted and at this point my destiny was forever changed.

However, much to my father's fury, my academic pursuits at school were a total failure. Since enrolling at Glasgow Academy in 1932, I had found more attractive diversions. Rugby, rifle shooting and the Officer Training Corps (OTC) were much more to my liking. My progress through the OTC saw me gain an 'A' certificate and become the company quartermaster sergeant. Such standing could qualify me for a commission in the Territorial Army, though in the immediate time frame it offered me treasured independence. With the assistance of a lone cadet corporal, I was tasked with managing the armoury. Responsible for hundreds of Lee Enfield .303 rifles, ammunition, uniforms and other related gear, the mix of responsibility and being left alone sat very well with me. The store was conveniently located adjacent to the school canteen and provided a very comfortable haven. Like myself, my young off-sider, Corporal Brown, was to find his wings in later life. Flying the powerful Hawker Typhoon, he would suffer an engine failure and land adjacent to the Brighton Pier. It was at this time that I became a very competent marksman, winning competitions at public school meets at Bisley and Territorial Army contests. It was a skill that was to serve me well in the subsequent years.

Though still a schoolboy, manhood seemed to be rapidly approaching and I needed to contemplate a career. With my successes in the OTC and on the rifle range, I initially contemplated the army as a choice. My father did not agree and, in retrospect, my poor academic results may well have precluded it as an option. It seemed very apparent to us all that war was looming and having viewed films such as 'All Quiet on the Western Front', a number of us figured that one seemed very vulnerable to artillery shells dropping on top of you as a member of the infantry. With fond memories of my flight at Abbotsinch, the Royal Air Force then caught my attention. A little wiser this time around, I did not inform my father of my military aspirations. Surreptitiously attending an interview, I was told that unless I lost weight and smartened up my mathematics I would be deemed unsuitable. My dear mother had supported me splendidly through many acrimonious disputes with my father and again she came to the fore, organising a 'crammer' to work with me on my mathematical shortcomings. To address the issue of my weight, I consulted a doctor who converted me to brown bread and prescribed a two mile run to be taken daily. The combination succeeded and my performance at a second interview gained my acceptance into the Royal Air Force. My father was far from impressed.

I reported for training as a pilot with No. 11 Elementary and Reserve Flying Training School at Perth on March 13th, 1939. My chief memory of that rather significant day is arriving absolutely frozen stiff, as I was driven to Scone airfield perched in the 'dickey seat' of my brother-in-law's open top Triumph. No time was wasted and the next day I was clipping around the sky with my first flying instructor, Flying Officer Sayers. The aircraft was the younger brother of the biplane from my youth; the venerable de Havilland DH82 Tiger Moth, which was to go on to carve its own legend training pilots throughout the Commonwealth. Intertwined with the joy of flight was the inevitable labour of knowledge. All forms of theory were foisted upon our course in the landlocked hours. In addition to the more subtle aspects of aerodynamics, navigation and meteorology, we were trained in the art of 'swinging' the propeller. In the days before starter motors, this was the technique for bursting one's aircraft into life by hand. We also received basic, practical instruction in the workings of all things mechanical. Aside from our engines, the training targeted the Vickers machine gun and the challenge of breaking it down and re-constructing it in two minutes. In accordance with the highest military traditions, our instructor was able to complete the task blindfolded. Two intensive weeks after arriving at Perth, I was solo with a grand total of 8 hours 45 minutes flying time under my belt.

My course contained a cross-section of the Commonwealth and was comprised of a number of Canadians, one Australian, an assortment of Britons and a former Palestinian policeman. Our colonial brothers tended be older than we natives and had backgrounds ranging from lumber jacks to undertakers and beyond. With such diverse heritages, it is little wonder that our course went close to being thrown out due to some extra-curricular activity.

The preceding course had held their departure party at a

local dance hall in Perth and, after several fights, had been summarily thrown out by the locals. Our wild colonial boys decided that the flying school's honour must be preserved. They intended to achieve this by clearing the dance hall of all the locals and called for the whole of our course to attend. Similar to my arrival at Scone, I was again transported at the mercy of the elements on the back seat of an open-top Singer Le Mans. In this instance, I also served as an auxiliary fuel pump, hanging over the back and blowing into the filler cap in an attempt to keep fuel moving to the engine. To further enhance the vapour's effects, the Canadians introduced me to my first beer. And second. And third. I found a cozy corner where I could hold a wall up, whilst my course mates set about 'cutting in' on the local girls. Predictably, if not predestined, a stoush ensued. As all hell broke loose, I found myself backed into my secure corner and on the receiving end of some unwanted attention. Fortunately for me, I was saved from a beating by one of our French Canadians, Badeaux, who was an expert fighter. Whereas I had been attempting to merely hold my aggressor at bay, Badeaux was able to send him on his way with a series of lusty blows. In the midst of the melee, our lookout warned us of the imminent arrival of the constabulary. We vacated the premises with due haste, only to be paraded by the chief flying instructor the following morning. In a hostile diatribe, he warned that if our lives were not blameless for the remainder of the course, we would be thrown out.

With such a threat hanging over us, we applied ourselves accordingly. On May 28th, 1939 with 25 hours solo and a matter of minutes more dual, I was assessed as 'above average' by the chief flying instructor at Perth. Logbook endorsed, I packed my bags and set course for Uxbridge where we were to be indoctrinated as short service commission pilots; acting pilot officers under probation. We were more commonly known as 'bog rats under suspicion'. Our flight lieutenant, guide and mentor was a one-legged World War One Royal Flying Corps veteran who was ably assisted by several corporals. The latter's main purpose seemed to be marching us at double time and giving us all variety of hell; though always addressing us as "Sir".

Our order of dress through this tirade was caps, sports jackets and flannels. This degree of relative conformity was in preparation of the arrival of our uniforms, for which we were given an allowance of fifty pounds. Uniforms could, in turn, be purchased from an approved list of suppliers. I selected a sanctioned tailor, Austin Reed. Unfortunately, on their arrival at the docks, our colonial lads had been suborned by Burtons, 'the fifty *shilling* tailor', who was definitely not on the list. This created a nasty situation for our aged flight lieutenant, however, he obviously won out and our comrades had to forego their tailoring profits and select an approved supplier. Even the suppliers of repute were still at the mercy of our leader. When the trucks bearing our uniforms arrived at Uxbridge, he would personally make the inspection of their wares and inherently give the suppliers unadulterated hell. Even so, fifty pounds bought a remarkable amount of gear. One best blue uniform with shoes, black socks, shirts and tie. One mess kit complete with wellington boots, greatcoat, camp bed, canvas wash basin, gaiters and other extraneous bits that one never had call to use. Now freshly kitted out, there was still a catch. At the beginning of the war, any losses of uniform through combat or accident were to be replaced by the owner at his expense. Unbelievably, this policy only changed in 1942 when battle dress was issued to wear on operations.

Bearing in mind our close call with the locals at Perth, our proximity and easy access to London provided a great temptation to our boys from the Colonies. They became very adept at breaking out of, and back into, camp at Uxbridge, much to the envy of we law abiding timid Brits who would cover for our mates at nightly roll call.

In June of 1939 my course was on the move again. This time to commence our advanced flying tuition at Hullavington, Wiltshire. My instructor was Sergeant 'Taffy' Morgan, a true Welshman, and the aircraft were all from the Hawker stable. My initial trainers at Hullavington were the dual-seat Hart and its bombing variant, the Audax. They were classic, open cockpit biplanes with the finest of lines and prepared me well for my first fighter; the single-seat Fury. An absolutely beautiful example of an aeroplane, streamlined and silver, it represented the pinnacle of biplane technology and aesthetics before progress saw the top wing cast off into history. The pedigree was also evident by the Vickers machine guns mounted on the nose in front of the cockpit. Reaching up to cock and fire this almost historic weaponry was reminiscent of the knights who had graced the skies in World War One. Through the chattering of the Vickers and the associated spray of oil, one could almost see the Maltese-crossed rudder of the Red Baron's triplane. Our days were filled with formation flying, gunnery, navigation and the many other skills of the trade.

It was during my time at Hullavington that I experienced one of my most uncomfortable flights. A little fatigued after a night out, I was tasked for an instructional navigation exercise in one of our Audax bombers. On such a sortie, one would be connected to the aircraft by a 'dog lead' to facilitate the tangled climb from the control seat down to the bombsight where 'wind sights' were taken and a navigation log kept. After each calculation one would climb back up and advise the instructor of the results and the next course to steer. In the early generation of trainer this communication was achieved by yelling down a rubber pipe, or 'Gosport tube', that was connected to the instructor's helmet. By the fourth leg of the trip, the climbing, calculating and yelling was taking its toll. I was becoming rather green around the gills. Fearing I couldn't continue, I advised the instructor, "I'm feeling sick!" and somewhere between the maze of rubber tubing and the roar of the airflow, my instructor heard, "Steer one three six!" As we peeled off to the south-east of England, far removed from where we should have been pointing, the terrain became somewhat in conflict with our charts. Nearing the coast and running out of England, my instructor realised that we were lost. Scanning the surrounding scenery for any clue we spotted an army camp, to which we flew and landed. My instructor climbed from the aircraft and made his way confidently to the nearby operations hut. Without approaching a soul, he located the notice board where he obtained our current position from the title on the station orders. Returning to the Audax, we calculated a course homeward and departed. Subsequently recognising his role in the debacle, I was given a rather good rating for the exercise and our detour remained strictly confidential.

Though we trained hard, it is not to say that there was no time for a reprieve. My best friend at Hullavington was 'Pissy' Edwards. The nickname was rather unfairly foisted upon him as his beer intake was actually quite moderate. Together with Pissy, I would go to Bath where we had struck up an acquaintance with an elderly actress who ran the renowned 'Hole in the Wall' pub. If we had missed the return train, she would allow us to doss down in the pub and we would catch the early morning 'milk train' which had us arrive just in time for parade. They were good times, but war loomed and there were to be tough times ahead, as Pissy would learn first hand. Later posted to a Fairey Battle squadron in France, he was shot down and taken prisoner in May 1940. The long confinement finally took its toll towards the end of the war. Only weeks before liberation, he stood up one day, walked to the barbed wire and started climbing through it. He was shot dead by the guard in broad daylight.

Leave was not always spent in London with Pissy, at other times I would head home to Bearsden and see my family. I was on one such leave, when I arrived home only to be greeted by a telegram that read, "Return Immediately!" I cursed my poor fortune, but didn't even pause or unpack before turning around and heading back to base. I was curious as to the urgency of my return and hoped it wasn't of a disciplinary nature. My curiosity was soon to be quelled. The date was September 3rd, 1939 and war had been declared in Europe.

As I made my way to Glasgow's central station, the city was already bathed in a dim blue light to mask it from would-be bombers. War had been coming for some time and no time was wasted in readying the nation. It seemed overnight that barrage balloons were hoisted, air raid shelters built and gas masks carried as standard clothing. This period was to become known as the 'Phoney War'. Hitler had torn through Poland with Blitzkrieg and we expected all hell to break loose on the home front; but nothing happened. The only bombing that took place was the dropping of millions of leaflets over Germany by British bombers warning the German public of the evils of Nazism. At war's end, RAF Bomber Command Chief, Air Marshal 'Bomber' Harris stated, "My personal view is that the only thing achieved was largely to supply the continent's requirements of toilet paper for the five long years of the war."

All manner of fate awaited our course in the dark years ahead. I qualified for my Wings on September 22nd, though I received only an 'average' rating endorsed with the comment, "Inaccurate in all departments of flying". Even so, it was at this point that we were selected for our speciality within the air force and much to my delight, I was chosen to fly fighters. To celebrate, along with Pissy Edwards, we were treated to a night on the town by our instructors. The evening featured a superb meal and the consumption of a significant number of ales, much to my detriment. We staggered back to the airfield and into the wooden huts that were our home where my conditioned worsened somewhat. Making for one of the open windows, I released the remnants of my dinner. Leaning from the window, I watched the rats scurrying around below and couldn't help but feel disappointment in wasting a rare dining experience.

With celebrations over, my training now focused on more and more formation training, aerobatics, low level sorties, quartering attacks and attacks from astern. By course-end in November I was becoming very confident in my domain and the upgraded assessment of 'above average' was now written in my log. With the princely total of 145 hours I was on my way to an operational squadron and to war.

CHAPTER THREE

Down to Earth

From flying school I was posted to a newly formed unit, 245 Squadron at Leconfield. The unit was so new, in fact, that we had no aircraft. Ironically, our motto was *Fugo Non Fugio* (I put to flight. I do not flee), a sentiment that we had no chance of enacting. All dressed up and ready to go, we awaited the arrival of something, anything, to fly.

We were originally quartered in an old wooden mess, while the final touches were applied to our new, more substantial digs. We shared the facility with an auxiliary air force unit, who were a group of larrikins. They were tremendous chaps, all young and full of character. Generally from well-to-do and university backgrounds, the auxiliary chaps' tunics were distinct from ours in that they were lined with scarlet silk.

In contrast from our relatively genteel approach to service life and adherence to mess etiquette, the aux lads were somewhat more free-spirited. Following the final evening's dining, our comrades set about demolishing the old mess. They literally tore the place apart. There were holes through walls that strongly resembled the outline of a rampant pilot and all manner of structures were reduced to components. It was one of the wildest parties to be seen and a rather lively farewell to our old accommodation.

Finally, after weeks of waiting, our first aircraft arrived in the form of Miles Magisters. The dual-seat, open-cockpit trainers were never going to win the war with a top speed of 110 knots and a total absence of armament. What they did offer was the opportunity to maintain our flying skills to some basic degree. With time, however, young pilots can become bored and this was to prove costly for two of our squadron mates. Whilst out one morning, simulating low level flight over the trenches, the two pilots of a Magister decided to effectively 'play chicken'. This was achieved by skimming along towards some fixed object and handing over control to the other pilot as late as possible. Should his nerve give out, the other pilot may take over control earlier, though this was effectively counted as a loss. Whilst tempting fate in this manner, they spotted the 'Flying Scotsman' roaring along the rails at speed, northwards towards Edinburgh. Flying down to ground level, the pilot in control positioned the Magister in formation with the luxury train at very close quarters. Aboard the train, excited passengers watched the display outside their windows. Ahead a stone wall came in to sight and was to prove a substantial obstacle. In keeping with their game, the call of "Over to you. You have control", was conveyed down the Gosport tube at the last possible moment. Unfortunately his mate did not hear the call and the Magister speared in, demolishing both the stone wall and the aircraft. Both pilots were dragged, badly injured, from the wreckage and conveyed to hospital. Neither ever returned to the squadron.

Shortly after our Magisters arrived we were equipped with our first combat aircraft, the Bristol Blenheim. The twin-engined medium bomber was an ergonomic nightmare with an array of levers and switches in the worst imaginable positions. Behind the pilot sat four switches; two for the propeller setting and two for cutting the engine. Reaching blindly back, one always feared selecting the wrong pair after take-off and leaving oneself with an absence of sound. Similarly the undercarriage and flap levers were between the seats and incorrect selection of gear instead of flaps had led to more than one aircraft gracefully kneeling down as it taxied in from the runway. This problem was addressed by placing a jagged-edged box around one lever and Blenheim pilots were subsequently identified by the tell-tale scar on the back of their hand. Such was the level of multi-engine aircraft technology at that time and it was with great relief that we were advised of the impending arrival of an advanced single-engined bomber, the Fairey Battle. As the squadron's only 'single-engined' pilot, I was to be sent to Abbotsinch to collect the sole dual-control Battle in the country. On its return, the aircraft would be used to convert our 'twin-engined' pilots to its ways with a minimum of pain. Well, that was the plan anyway.

On arriving at Abbotsinch, the site of my first flight as a

schoolboy, I was instructed to gain some experience on the Battle. This consisted of the rather standard, single take-off and landing with an instructor before being left to one's own devices. I subsequently proceeded to undertake a series of handling exercises which included a generous number of low level 'beat ups' of places of personal interest. My favourite was to roar along Bardowie Loch and flip dinghies with my propwash. When not beating up dinghies or my friends' homes, I was also partial to cutting the grass around the neighbouring mountainous regions. Here the only folk to disturb were waiting to be shorn. I was happily familiarising myself with the Battle by day and my home town by night, when I received a call from my CO back at Leconfield. In no uncertain terms he enquired as to the whereabouts of *his* aeroplane and informed me that I should deliver it to him post-haste. I hurriedly threw my kit together and clambered into my new steed to convey it to its new home. It was February 10th, 1940 and the weather surrounding the airfield was bleak and foggy as I lifted off and started into the climb. I groped my way through the murk before finally popping out on top of the fog. What greeted my eyes took my breath away; I was surrounded by a mass of bobbing barrage balloons. Through sheer good fortune I had escaped harm at the hands of the helium-filled defence system, climbing up amongst the lethal cables that tethered them to the environs of Glasgow. A few years later I would witness the lethal potential of barrage balloons as they dotted the skies over Crewe. One of our own, a Shorts Stirling, flew into the cables, exploding into a fireball before falling to earth and killing the entire crew.

With the near-miss behind me and my heart still racing, I set course for Leconfield. Passing Thornton Hill, I had begun to relax when my engine spluttered. It coughed again and then failed. This was particularly embarrassing as I was not at a great height at the time and confronted with extremely limited options. It had been a very hard winter and the small rolling foothills were snow coated with a deeply frozen core of soil beneath. Without further ado I chose a field ahead which was divided by a small track crossing it and terminated with a house and garage at the far end. Not ideal, but it would have to do. Setting my speed and lining up on the clearing, I experienced a very uncomfortable feeling. The Battle was the first aircraft I had flown with retractable undercarriage and the proximity of the ground without my wheels lowered was rather unnerving. My next action seemed logical at that moment, but with the benefit of hindsight and experience, it was a basic error. I lowered the undercarriage.

I impacted the frozen earth well into the chosen landing site and bounced high above the snow. Floating over the track that I had noted on approach, my eyes caught those of a woman pushing a pram with a baby in it and we looked at each other in mutual disbelief. I touched down again and this time I stuck. Surmounting the crest of the hill, I started down at a great rate before striking a hedge which served to shear off my main wheels. The aircraft fell to its belly with little loss in speed initially and was now effectively a Royal Air Force toboggan heading straight for the residence's garage. I tried to gain some directional control by kicking the rudders, though this proved very ineffective other than to slew the aircraft slightly from side to side. Throughout, the Battle's course remained true. As I contemplated whether I would stop in time, one of the shed's double doors opened and a head protruded to take in proceedings. The head was then rapidly withdrawn and reappeared through a side door, at speed, with body firmly attached. Fortunately my speed washed off and I slid to a halt with my starboard wing totally blocking, but somehow not touching, the garage doors. Sitting there I was overcome with another wave of trepidation. It was not fear of fire or explosion that gripped me, it was an administrative oversight. In my haste to depart I had failed to sign the aircraft out and consequently the flight wasn't on squadron records; a cardinal sin. I hastily made a call to my point of departure, where an accommodating sergeant was able to complete the 'Form 700' using artistic licence and a signature from one of my old flight authorisations.

The residents at the scene of my less-than-grand entrance were a family by the name of Moore. They were very good to me considering my unusual and somewhat threatening arrival. Their attitude may well have been tempered by Mr Moore's background as a World War One fighter pilot. In his Sopwith Camel he had been one of the original 'Knights of the Air', duelling over the mud-bound trenches of France against the likes of Richthofen's Flying Circus. Those romantic days of chivalry must have seemed a distant memory as my legless Fairey Battle sat forlornly at his shed's entrance. With great empathy they invited me in and offered me lunch and hot chocolate. From the strangest of situations, a friendship grew and I subsequently maintained contact with the family, even after they had moved to the suburbs of Edinburgh. Their daughter, Kitty, particularly caught my eye. She went on to join the Women's Royal Naval Service and be stationed at Turnhouse; just a short flight from my base at Leconfield.

The Battle ended up precluding the use of the garage for about a week as the recovery crew set about its salvage. It seems that I had not been the first to be bitten by and, in turn 'bend', this single-engined bomber as Mr Moore overheard the crew comment, "Thank God someone has done a good job on it. This makes the second time we've picked it up." For 245 Squadron it meant the absence of their single-engine bomber come trainer. For me, it meant the wrath of the CO and a short time on the Blenheim, accumulating twin-engine hours and earning my tell-tale laceration.

Finally, in March of 1940 our squadron was equipped with the Hawker Hurricane Mk I. With it, the Hurricane brought the dawn of a new era for the Royal Air Force. As beautiful as the lines of the Hawker biplanes were, they were both the pinnacle and the end of their generation. It was envisaged, quite correctly, that the next epoch of aerial warfare would be conducted at high speed with limited time for short, sharp bursts of exchange between fighters. The new design called for speed and substantial firepower to ensure sufficient lethal strikes upon an enemy. The Hurricane provided the first step in this direction and the aircraft would ultimately prove to be the backbone, if not the 'poster boy', of Britain's darkest hour.

Demolishing the mess wasn't the only hair-raising experience in 245 Squadron's time at Leconfield. The airfield was a grass field with a rise situated in its midst. The Spitfire squadron that co-habited with us sat beyond the rise and were invisible to our operation; as we were to theirs. The first one would be aware of a Spitty scramble would be the roar of Merlins followed by the sight of the squadron coming over the rise, tails up and about to take flight. It was quite impressive, unless they'd scrambled our Hurricane squadron at the same time! In that event, we would be roaring towards each other, throttles wide and destined for disaster. After a number of close calls we devised a highly technical system of keeping to the left, or something similar. In the absence of Air Traffic Control, we avoided coming to grief in this way, though one's heart was always in one's mouth until the rise was successfully cleared.

To compound matters, Scottish weather had subjected the field to a drought which was in time broken by a tremendous downpour. The result was a waterlogged mire. A genius amongst us devised a plan to cover the field in crushed peat. The sticky black remains of broken-down vegetation was smeared over our airfield in order to miraculously absorb the water and provide us with a sealed surface from which to take off and land. The actual result was for the black clag to be thrown up by the spinning airscrew as we set full power for take-off and straight into our radiators! With our engine barely able to breathe, we lacked full boost for the take-off run and only just managed to claw our way into the air. Staggering clear of the trees at the perimeter, the engine temperatures started to climb through the roof. Barely aloft with a dying engine, we would make due haste to throw our machines back on the ground. Needless to say, the peat was returned to the bogs from whence it came.

Our issues with Leconfield were not to last long as the squadron was on the move. Our orders came through and we were being re-deployed to the south-east. The war had arrived for 245 Squadron.

CHAPTER FOUR

Into the Fray

May 28th saw 245 Squadron move to its new base at Hawkinge. Perched on the coast near the white cliffs of Dover, only the Channel now separated us from the German advance. We commenced operations over the Dunkirk evacuation immediately and two days later were scrambled to intercept some Dornier 17s over the French coast. Unfortunately they made a dash for it and slipped away, which wasn't overly surprising as the German bombers were generally quite fast. The only ones we stood much of a chance chasing down were the Ju88 and He111s. Matters were complicated by the need to 'pull the tit' to cross the Channel with minimum delay. This involved pulling a small lever on the instrument panel that boosted our available power. We'd boost an extra four pounds, from eight to twelve, leading to not only an increase in speed but also an increase in fuel burn. Operating at the limit of our endurance anyway, this only left ten to fifteen minutes operationally over France and made the return flight even more marginal.

As a consequence, our patrol returned over the English coast very low on fuel under the duress of miserable weather having been aloft for two and a half hours. At the very limit of the Hurricane's endurance, with Squadron Leader Eric Whitley and Flight Lieutenant 'Ginge' Mowat, I had diverted to Kenley whilst two or three others of our flight had been forced to put down on England's green fields. Fortunately, we three had arrived in time for lunch at the mess and celebrated our arrival on vapours with a few ales. Aside from this glimpse of some Dornier 17s, the patrols had been inconclusive. There seemed to me to be a distinct lull in the air war that we had been sent to fight, though May 31st was to be a different story altogether.

My tangle with the Me109s that day had led to my 'outlanding' at Dunkirk and my trek back to friendly shores. Downed on foreign soil in the midst of combat, I had no grasp of what was coming next. A mere teenager, I was face to face with the realities of the ground war. In all honesty, I had hoped that joining the RAF would have spared me from the horror. The war films of schoolboy days were still a recent memory as I watched our Spitfires plunge headlong into the water and the dead Tommys float on the swell. There was no doubting that I had now entered the fray.

As I trudged along the French shore, my armourer and fitter hung their legs over an English cliff and scanned the skies for the return of their Hurricane and its pilot. The consensus of the other pilots back at the squadron was that I was a goner, yet my 'erks' didn't lose hope and waited faithfully. They were probably still sitting there when *The Golden Eagle* docked at Margate and I called the duty officer at Hawkinge, Pilot Officer Hill. By coincidence, he was also the squadron parachute officer and I advised him that I still had my trusty silk in hand, feeling rather guilty about not actually having an aeroplane. He had shared the squadron's view of my fate and was genuinely surprised to hear from me and sent transport for me without further ado. Back at the base I checked in my parachute only to be told that it was a write-off as a result of the glycol, oil and fuel in which it had been doused. Once again I slung it over my shoulder, though it seemed more like I was joined at the hip with this piece of equipment. I finally packaged it up and posted it to my mother at Bearsden.

De-briefed by the intelligence officer, I made a sorry sight in my oil-stained uniform and, as a consequence, was given the next day off to organise a replacement. There is no way that I had the funds to purchase new kit, though I did have sufficient resources to take my erks to Dover to celebrate my safe return and hold a wake for their Hurricane. Grateful to be alive, I set about sharing a few beers with my boys when we attracted the attention of some of our army brethren. They proceeded to enquire of us where the Royal Air Force was to be found, as they were convinced it was nowhere to be seen in the skies over Dunkirk. Whilst I begged to differ, my erks took distinct exception to the inference and informed them that they had first hand knowledge of the RAF's presence at Dunkirk. In particular, my portion of air power was being lapped by the

French surf as we spoke. As the situation escalated to an unhealthy point, I intervened and settled the parties down. We returned to our celebrations, but it was obvious that tensions were running high.

Back at Hawkinge after my short reprieve, it was operations as normal. The day would start before dawn and inevitably kick off with a cup of tea. We had thirty minutes to get dressed and make our way to dispersal where we gave our aircraft and equipment a thorough checking over. Routine complete, we now waited at the ready, knowing that at any time we could be called into action by the shrill ring of the operations hut phone that would order us to scramble. In these idle times, we would suppress any apprehension or negativity that may be creeping up from within. Each individual went about their own routine; smoking pipes, leaning back in deck chairs or playing informal games of cricket. Others played cards for phenomenal stakes. Debts of millions were racked up as the odds were against actually surviving to have to pay up. For me, my pastime was sleep. Purely and simply. I was able to doze regardless of the situation or time of day. I'd stretch out on the grass near the ops hut and drift off, far from the madding skies. It would relax me and prepare my body and soul for the turmoil it may be called to confront at any moment. I didn't contemplate the future, or relive the past; I just slept.

Then the call would come; scramble! My eyes would open and I'd fly to my feet. At this time there was absolutely no fear as I ran to my aircraft, concentrating on not tripping over. Climbing into the cockpit, plugging in the R/T, strapping on my helmet, parachute and safety straps. With a thumbs up to the ground crew, magnetos on, battery OK and a press of the starter button the Merlin would shake and then explode into life. Gauges would come to life and I'd wave away the battery cart and chocks; we'd be on our way. From slumber to slipstream in less than two minutes.

June 2nd left me little time to dedicate to slumber. First up there was a photo call for the squadron's various flights. I took my place, seated in the front row in a photo that survives to this day. Still looking a little stunned from my misadventure, my uniform bears the numerous oily marks that were impregnated as my Hurricane bled to death. Posterity captured, it was back into a Hurricane and bound for the French coast on an offensive patrol with my flight commander, Ginger Mowat.

Forty-eight hours after having my aircraft shot to shreds, I was again sitting over the English Channel. Not quite as cocksure as the lad I had been, I swiveled my head around and scanned the skies. I was not going to be caught out twice. Looking for the enemy, we swept the Dunkirk area without success. We did, however, fly down a stretch of beach just to the north-east of the township and near the Belgian border. There, forlornly sat R-DX parallel to the coast at the mid-tide line, destined to be eventually submerged with the changing tides and passage of time.

With the exception of a few days at Turnhouse in Edinburgh, Hawkinge was my home for the month of June. In this time I flew another thirty or so sorties comprising of scrambles, convoy patrols, offensive patrols and bomber patrols. More often than not, the latter operations were a misadventure with the bomber rendezvous being missed or briefings altered at the latest possible moment. Even so, it was a busy time.

Having completed an uneventful offensive patrol over France I led my section back across the Channel. Sitting at relatively low level over the waves and approaching home, I noticed the disturbing trend of my oil temperature climbing. On the Merlin this was always a worrying development requiring immediate attention. I reduced power to the minimum I could get by with and opened the radiator fully to maximise the cooling airflow. I radioed my section and they throttled back to keep in formation with me. Still the temperature continued to soar. Low, slow and vulnerable, it was with tremendous relief that we crossed the friendly coast and fortunately, the V12 engine hung together long enough for me to land at Hawkinge.

Climbing out of the cockpit I related the symptoms to the ground crew who set about diagnosing the problem. It was not long until the reason for the 'overtemping' engine became obvious. There was substantial damage found where the wing joined the fuselage, the wing root. Something had punched a very clean hole, through not only my wing's leading edge, but also the oil tank located therein. I was in somewhat of a quandary as I didn't recall encountering any ground fire and the temperature had begun to rise when I was well clear of German guns. On further investigation, a bloody pulp was found in my oil tank. It was the remains of a bird which I had struck, probably on the wave-hopping trip home. Even so, it had nearly brought me down as surely as a German bullet.

'Real' anti-aircraft fire and flak were constant companions.

Occasionally one would pass so close that the air rush of the projectile could be heard above the noise of the Merlin engine. Fortunately, the shell did not detonate at that time, but ventured forth and exploded at a higher altitude. Still I received flak damage on occasions, as did my New Zealand-born commanding officer, Squadron Leader Eric Whitley. We were on patrol over France when we encountered very heavy anti-aircraft fire. In the midst of bursts of flak exploding around us, the CO broke our standard tight formation and proceeded to wheel about the sky in a series of wild aerobatic manoeuvres. We were unable to contact him over the never-reliable TR9D, though on this occasion the radio unit wasn't the problem. Finally, his aircraft righted itself and a flurry of hand signals from the leader called us back into formation. It transpired that red hot shrapnel had shot through his canopy, slicing his oxygen mask and microphone. The culprit then proceeded to settle, sizzling between his collar and the tender flesh on the back of his neck. Fighting to dislodge the agonising piece of molten metal he had subsequently lost effective control of his aircraft until the shrapnel was removed. A significant burn to the back of his neck bore testimony to his experience.

Squadron Leader Whitley would go on to be Mentioned in Despatches and win the Distinguished Service Order (DSO) whilst flying in the Western Desert. However, it was in his time with 245 Squadron that he was awarded the Distinguished Flying Cross (DFC) for leading a successful raid on a Luftwaffe base in France. The attack was crafted by Whitley organising the tactics and co-ordination with other section leaders. They set out and hit the airfield at Rouen-Boos in a daring low level attack, putting paid to around fifty enemy fighters. The Hurricanes skimmed the trees and cut loose with the Brownings. At not much more than eye height, they were able to see deep into the hangars and one such structure seemed to house a number of German personnel lined up on what may have been a 'pay parade' or similar. Their fate was akin to that of the fighters stranded on the flightline.

We also suffered losses. On June 1st, the day after my own fateful encounter, we lost two of our pilots. They were young Irishmen, Alan Treanor and Robert West. 'Pengy' West was a good friend of mine and earned his nickname by his resemblance to the wee sea-bird. On the day of my demise over Dunkirk, he'd shared the common belief that I was lost for good and had grabbed my best shirt collar from my kit. Pengy was wearing this when he was shot down the following day, though there was no cross-channel home-coming for my Irish chum. I was now down to a single collar, though more to the point; I had lost a comrade in arms.

We also lost our sole Bristol Blenheim at this time. The aircraft was a tremendous 'squadron hack' that we could fill up and move people around the countryside at will. The Blenheim departed one morning to pick up our chief engineer at Blackpool. Shortly after take-off on the return flight, it lost an engine and plunged into the sea. Speculation was that the treacherous propeller and engine cutout switches had claimed another victim. This was particularly feasible as the engine seemed to fail at the very time when the pilot would be attempting to set the props from fine to coarse pitch.

For all the fury in the sky and my numerous sweeps over France, aside from Dunkirk, I had only one other combat with German fighters in my time at Hawkinge. On June 25th, Flight Lieutenant Thompson led six of us and, as before, I was at the head of the rear section as fighter cover and flying at 25,000 feet, or 'Angels 25'. With new found motivation, my eyes were in constant motion as I scanned the skies for the enemy. Just off the French coast, near Cherbourg, I spotted three aircraft below climbing at an extremely high rate. They were passing from our left to right, parallel to the shoreline and I was sure they had seen us. I warned our leader several times, but the dreaded TR9D was true to form yet again. It was obvious Thompson hadn't spotted them as they climbed through our level to gain the advantage of altitude. The trio then started into a starboard turn to position on a track opposite to our own. My eyes were locked on them as it was obvious that they were positioning for an assault. And then it came. Wheeling into a diving turn they launched a starboard rear quarter attack. I cranked hard into a right hand turn to engage the leader head on. He recognised my intentions and inexplicably turned away to break off the attack. This served to present me with a textbook full deflection shot as he crossed in front of me, from right to left. I heaved the Hurricane to the left to take the shot. Pulling heavy 'g's' at altitude, the Hurricane was holding on to flight by its fingernails and within a hair's breadth of stalling. Laying off a gunsight's width, I fired. The tracers streaked to the target and the De Wilde ammunition hit and sparkled as my shots worked their way down the entire length of his port side. My angle made for good penetration of the .303's and I knew I had him as he started down, though my attention was immediately drawn back to my own deteriorating predicament. The recoil from my firing guns had knocked the last puff of aerodynamics from my fighter's wings. I stalled and flicked into a spin. Knowing that my foe's two chums were still around, I let the aircraft spin and made my way for a cloud bank below. Out the other side, I recovered from the spin and tentatively climbed back through the cloud in search of the other Huns. As so often happens, within minutes of aerial combat the hostile sky was now empty. Most of my formation had been taken by surprise and scattered accordingly. The remaining pair of Germans had continued on when the leader broke off and, as a consequence, damaged two of our machines. One being that of Flight Lieutenant Thompson.

Back on the ground at Hawkinge we made our way to the intelligence officer to detail our encounter. There was some uncertainty about the identity of the enemy, whether they were Me109s or the much debated Heinkel 113s; I went with the consensus of He 113s. As we waited to make our reports, our leader was lamenting the damage to his parachute as it had a bullet lodged in it. For my part, our rigid definition of a kill precluded me making a claim. I had not seen the enemy aircraft crash, catch fire or explode. Wearily, I underwent my intelligence de-briefing and submitted a combat report. It had been a long day; I trudged back to my bunk, lay down and slept.

CHAPTER FIVE

Errors of Judgement

The silver gilt rose Battle of Britain clasp that emblazons the ribbon of the 1939-45 Star is a highly prized emblem. The requirement is for the recipient to have flown at least a single operational fighter sortie between two rather arbitrarily chosen dates. Those who fought know that the Battle of Britain was far more than the three months highlighted by the clasp which we proudly wear. From July 1940, the skies of south-eastern England filled with weaving contrails and spiralling, earthbound plumes of smoke as the aerial armadas clashed. The battle and its outcome is now a part of history, yet in the desperation of the finest hour, 245 Squadron was to bid farewell to Hawkinge.

When advised of the move, our CO anticipated that the airfield would soon cop a pounding and made it a priority to empty the cellar rather than see it blown up. To make an event of the farewell, showgirls were organised from some of London's clubs such as The Windmill. With arrangements in place and dusk approaching, the dreaded ops phone rang and my section was scrambled. Within minutes we were formed up over the Channel and setting course. Our sortie took us south of Calais where it was reported that there was a ground fight going on as the Germans attempted to winkle out some of our boys. As we combed the skies, there was no sign of the Luftwaffe and we imagined that they were probably off celebrating, given recent events. With fuel at a premium, we headed home to Hawkinge where we had missed the girls' show, however, like good pilots we played our part in the cellar's demise. Our old airfield was to stand at the Battle's doorstep and the CO's prediction would come true. On the day of our departure for Scotland, Hawkinge was strafed by the ever-bolder Luftwaffe.

Leconfield was little more than a transit stop for the pilots, aircraft and crew as our new home was to be RAF Aldergrove, eighteen miles north-west of Belfast in Northern Ireland. Moving the squadron as the Battle of Britain was approaching its pinnacle seemed at odds with requirements, but the powers-that-be had concerns elsewhere. With a change in geography came a change in role for the squadron. Our new task was effectively two pronged. Firstly, we assumed a training role for new pilots who were in turn posted to 11, 12 and 13 Groups at the forefront of the Battle. Secondly, we were operationally tasked to guard the British back door and the shipping that plied its routes. Our task was tinged with repetition and frustration, though we were also in Northern Ireland for a clandestine purpose should the war turn against us.

Our main operational role out of Aldergrove was to catch the Focke-Wulf Condors. The FW200 was the military development of a pre-war four-engined, long-range airliner. With its extensive range, armament and turn of speed, it proved an excellent escort for the German Navy, or *Kriegsmarine*. Following the fall of France, the Condors turned their attention to our shipping routes to the north-west. Able to attack shipping with great effect in its own right, the Condor increased its lethality, as it orchestrated attacks from the dreaded U-Boats.

Again our Hurricanes were operating at the limit of their range in order to patrol the distant waters of the supply routes. Whilst the Condor was in its realm, we were on much thinner ice. Our standard patrols had no effect as the Condors would see us coming and then simply stand out to sea, well beyond the range of our Hurricane's guns, until we were forced to head for home. With no radar to detect intruders, our response to calls for help was purely reactive and there existed little hope of ever making it to the action in time.

Scrambled from Aldergrove, we would take the shortest route, cutting across the west coast of Ireland and race to the distressed shipping. To further hasten our arrival, we'd 'pull the tit'. Unfortunately, this inevitably led to increased fuel consumption and further eroded our time to guard the shipping once we'd arrived. Enroute we often received unwanted attention in the form of 'ack ack' from our own navy's escort vessels.

With so many factors working against us, the best we ever seemed to achieve was to get there in time to see a Condor disappearing into the western sky at a speed too great for us to overhaul, though I did manage to just get a shot at our foe once.

Void of a centralised control, we were frequently called to arms by vigilant citizens. This morning the local postmaster in a little village beside Belfast Loch yelled down the phone, "We've been bombed! What are you going to do about it?" We scrambled ourselves and darted off at very low altitude. It was a lousy day with low cloud and snow, making the hills we needed to cross virtually impassable. I managed to squeeze my section through a small gap and on clearing the hills we spotted a Condor. It was immediately obvious that he had seen us as he made straight up for the cover of the clouds. I pulled my nose up to follow him and let loose with a burst at an incredibly long range. My first thoughts being that the shots would be more disturbing to the township below than the German. Like a horse slightly irritated by a fly, the Condor whisked into cloud and vanished.

Our dance with the Condors was frustrating and repetitive so in a bid to improve our odds, I put my head together with Whitley and Bowes-Hamilton, our intelligence officer. In company with the CO, we explored the western Scottish coastline around Oban and Port Ellen in one of the squadron's Magisters. We were looking for suitable fields that could not only accommodate a Hurricane, but were elevated enough to provide a sound vantage point to scan the skies to Ireland's north. With the landing sites located, we set about parking our Hurricanes there and waited, binoculars in hand. A far cry from radar, it was the best system we could devise at the time. Unfortunately, all of this planning bore no fruit. We continued to arrive at the convoy, having dodged the Southern Irish Air Force patrols, only to find ships on fire and sinking. The naval escorts continued to ignore our friendly identification signals and opened furious fire upon our Hurricanes.

The friendly fire emphasised the fragility of the situation in wartime. Whilst encounters with the enemy could very quickly see you meeting your maker, there were numerous other means of courting peril. Even in the 'safer' role of training, tragedy was always close at hand. We lost two pilots in an accident over Kitson and then a young Irishman who hailed not far from Aldergrove. Like so many others, he was receiving fighter training with 245 Squadron before heading off to the big show in the south-east. On a crisp, clear morning we were undertaking a formation take-off and the new recruit was sitting at position number three to my lead, back over my left shoulder. We opened our throttles and accelerated across the field in a tidy 'Vic' formation. On gaining flying speed, we proceeded to 'unstick' and the ground began falling away with our noses pointing skyward. To my horror, the young Irishman's aircraft continued to raise its nose further and further towards the vertical with his speed, the very lifeblood of flight, decaying rapidly. Peeling high and away to my left, the Hurricane painted a smooth unending arc until it was hurtling, nose down at the earth with no possibility of recovery. Before my eyes, man and machine impacted in a horrendous fireball.

The trainee pilot had met his end as the result of a relatively simple error. Prior to take-off the 'trim' was set to reduce the need for excessive physical strength in controlling the aircraft in the fore and aft. With the trim set fully aft, the nose continued to rise with force that the young man was unable to counter. The elevator trim is a small, simple wheel on the cockpit's wall. Set by turning, it could be easily overlooked by a newcomer, however, such small oversights can easily prove fatal. We chose to farewell our comrade with a traditional Irish wake which required the recently departed to be in attendance. Accordingly, his coffin was leant up in the corner, but due to the nature of his injuries, the casket was kept closed.

Not long afterwards, I lost my regular Hurricane at Aldergrove to a rather bizarre practice drill, known as 'battle climb'. It involved the pilot going full tilt to get the Hurri up to 15,000 feet where he subsequently flew for a period of time. A relatively straightforward exercise, however it was flown sans oxygen! Without oxygen, a pilot at altitude suffers from hypoxia and a number of physiological symptoms surface. Vision turns to black and white. Nail beds and lips turn blue. Lethargy creeps up and judgement becomes non-existent. All the while the pilot can be blissfully unaware and, if left unattended, lose consciousness and ultimately leave this mortal coil.

So it was at Aldergrove as our new chum set off in my aircraft to do battle with the oxygen-rarified upper atmosphere. In contrast, I took the opportunity to sit back and read the paper. A little while later the peace was broken by the sound of

a rapidly approaching Merlin. I raised my eyes in time to catch
sight of the Hurricane in a high speed vertical dive, spearing
head-long into Loch Ney. A totally useless waste of life and
bitterly ironic as breathing a hundred per cent oxygen became
standard from take-off to landing when I later ventured into
night operations.

Our role also involved tutoring experienced pilots who
lacked operational experience on the Hawker Hurricane
before being farmed out to the hard pressed squadrons in the
south-east. Many of these chaps were foreign nationals from
France and Poland. On one occasion, I was leading two Polish
pilots on a training exercise out over the Irish Sea when we
spotted an unidentified twin-engined aircraft below us, whose
form was totally unfamiliar to me. My two compatriots then
began a very loud exchange in Polish over the radio, none of
which I understood. Seconds later, they broke formation,
pulled their 'tits' and dived towards the cruising transport.
Having come from the 'old school' where you identified your
target prior to firing, this development was worrying, so I
rolled my Hurricane down and after the Poles. Recognising
their intention to attack, I sped my Hurricane as fast as it
would travel and edged my way ahead of my enthusiastic
friends where I was able to spot the boldly painted RAF
roundels on the mystery aircraft's fuselage. I desperately tried
to wave off the eager fighters in company with some fierce
expression over the airwaves. Finally, they comprehended my
actions and broke off the attack and it's just as well they did.
The aircraft was an early model Boston and was out over the
British countryside undertaking flight testing. Unaware of his
near miss with fate, the Boston landed at my base at
Aldergrove. On my return I quietly made a few discreet
enquiries as to the origins and activities of the twin-engined
American-built bomber. It transpired that at the helm was
Edward Donaldson, later Air Commodore Edward Donaldson
DSO, AFC and Bar who would go on to set a world speed
record in the jet age.

An American-built bomber that didn't fare as well was a
Lockheed Hudson, though the enemy in this case was not over-
enthusiastic allied pilots, but the cold Irish weather. In the midst
of winter's grip, the preflight inspection had failed to detect the
ice building up on the aircraft prior to it lining up for take-off.
The normally efficient curves of the wing's surface were

corrupted by ice. Speeding along the runway the pilot tried in vain to haul the ship into the air. With an overrun looming, he yanked the ice-laden Hudson into the air, but was unable to claw any altitude from the useless frozen planks protruding from his aeroplane. Inevitably, the speed washed off and the aircraft stalled to earth, impacting on the barracks at Aldergrove with a substantial loss of life. As was the way in wartime, details of the tragedy were siphoned off into a void and never really became general knowledge.

August 28th, 1940 saw me achieve the ripe old age of twenty. No mean feat in the world we were living in. For my birthday, I was once again in a Hurricane, in formation. As a flight leader, Ginge Mowat often instilled discipline by flying his section below high tension power lines, sagging mid-sections and all. On this occasion, I was number two in the vic to Ginge, with Pennington at number three. The flight was uneventful, though Ginge wanted to make the arrival particularly tight and we tucked in behind his wings for the landing. In such close proximity, it is essential for the leader to give notice of his pre-landing intentions as the lowering of wheels and flaps will slow his aircraft down decidedly. Turning in towards the field he called, "Wheels down. Now." We complied and maintained our small, critical spacing as the airfield lay ahead. Something must have distracted Ginge, or perhaps he just forgot, but there was no sign of his flaps lowering as the perimeter of Aldergrove rapidly approached. Then he remembered. Without notice, he dropped his flaps which had the same effect as slamming on the brakes from my perspective. We were just about to touch down when my propeller started chewing through the wingtip of Ginge's Hurricane, with the net effect of disintegrating the ends of my prop. We landed as a tangled mess. My wheels were no sooner rolling than the aircraft began to lurch to starboard and toward 'Penny'. My first thought was a blown tyre, but I soon realised I was being dragged down by Penny's wing which had climbed up onto mine. It was about to get very ugly, very quickly, when the other Hurricane's wing slid off mine and I was able to right my machine, eventually bringing it to a halt.

Ginge Mowat was a New Zealander and a little older then Pennington and I. Following the incident, as 'B' Flight commander, he generously gave Penny and I leave to celebrate my birthday in Bearsden. We could hardly pack quickly

enough, given our unexpected windfall. Surprisingly, when we
returned a week later, the inquiry into the landing incident had
already been held. We hadn't been called to give evidence and
no official mention of the collision was to surface again. One
can only wonder at the timing of such generosity.

Formation training made up a high proportion of our early
fighter training and was the cornerstone of fighter command
philosophy. Unfortunately, the all-consuming obsession with
formation, formation, formation was to prove costly and not
merely in the context of training at Aldergrove. It was after a
substantial period of time and a number of bitter experiences
that I came to a fundamental assessment of our strategy. The
entire approach to fighter tactics at the commencement of
World War Two was flawed.

Stemming from aerial combat of The Great War, tight
formation was necessary to allow the section to communicate
using hand signals. Even so, when the air battle erupted it was
every man for himself and a 'dogfight' ensued. The advent of
radio communications negated the need to fly in each others
pocket, yet we continued to fly formation in tight sections.
With the vic of three forming the base unit, the section, our
compact little v's were ideal for airshows, not modern combat.
Be it fighter-to-fighter or attacking bombers, flight at such close
quarters increased the risk of collision and committed us to
slow steady movements, which made us vulnerable targets. The
situation was aggravated by the demands of such flying. In a
vic, when the leader wasn't trying to avoid flying into the
section in front of him, he was responsible for looking for the
enemy ahead. Meanwhile, as the other two in the section
jostled to tuck in behind the leader's wings, they were
supposedly responsible for keeping a lookout behind. There we
were, a neat little parcel saying, "Come and get us." And with
no-one watching, get us they did.

At the same time, our foe was adopting a thoroughly
different approach. Tried, tested and true through the Spanish
Civil War and the subsequent Blitzkrieg, our opponents hunted
in a 'Finger Four' made up of two pairs. Unlike our rigid
sections trapped in straight and level flight, the Luftwaffe
fighters swept around the sky in an unrestrained, fluid motion.
They were constantly able to check their tails for any
approaching fighter and were not locked into any predictable
manoeuvres. They would fill the sky with a gaggle of pairs

making them efficient predators and difficult prey.

It was a bloody lesson learnt the hard way to an extreme and too many men died at the hands of poor strategy. We were practicing antiquated, suicidal methods whilst our enemy had recognised the dawn of modern aerial combat. I don't remember any specific edict changing our approach, but many of those who had been on the receiving end in France started to unofficially adopt the enemy's style. We also needed heavier armament as the Browning guns would often ricochet off the enemy if the angle wasn't right to penetrate. The Hurricane was later equipped with four 20mm cannons and these packed the punch to create terminal damage when the shots landed.

Throughout this endless period of frustration at Aldergrove, we were held in readiness for an operational role that fortunately was never needed; the destruction of the Irish Air Force. The task had been drafted on the eventuality of a German invasion of England and Southern Ireland. Fears of Southern Ireland surrendering its neutrality and aligning with the Axis forces were very real at the time. Years later, whilst at staff college, I would be shown a pier on the Irish coast which I was informed had been used to supply German U-Boats. In the midst of such tensions we had been briefed how to ensure the destruction of Ireland's air force though, luckily, the situation never came to pass. This was much to the relief of our own Irish pilots who, like so many of their countrymen, had nobly volunteered to serve with the British forces.

My time in Ireland came to a close, along with the year of 1940. My next posting was to the newly re-formed 96 Squadron at Cranage, near Crewe and I was permitted to borrow a Magister to make my way to England. Departing Aldergrove and crossing the Irish Sea was fine, but as I approached the English coast it was obvious that conditions were far from ideal. The moist coastal air had melded with the opaque industrial smoke of Merseyside, resulting in a good old pea-soup fog that extended well inland.

The famed Blackpool Tower stood above the murk and allowed me an opportunity to fix my position. Cranage was fogged out, as was the nearest alternative, Squires Gate. With daylight rapidly abandoning me, my options were disappearing at speed when a hole began to break in the fog, just north of Blackpool. I wheeled the Magister over the break and sighted a small, boggy field below. Before the opening had an opportunity to close, I flew the Magister down and prepared for yet another unscheduled landing. Peering through the poor visibility I guided the little trainer down, completing my pre-landing checks as I went. With a landing in the field ahead assured, I shut the engine down and watched the propeller come to a halt in a horizontal pose. Washing the speed off, I touched down without event and rolled across the lush pasture. In doing so, the small wheels of the 'Maggie' began to become inundated with mud, mud and yet more mud. Whilst serving to slow the aircraft down, the bogged wheels eventually seized up to such a degree that instead of merely stopping, the Magister ever so gently toppled forward to come to rest on its nose. With the propeller safely stopped, fortunately no damage was caused. I unstrapped and made my way to signs of civilisation where I was able to call the RAF station at Squires Gate and organise a bed for the night.

The next day, an engineering crew led by a flight sergeant, or 'Chiefy', had arrived at the scene and removed the mud-catching fairings from the Maggie's wheels. On my arrival, I climbed in and fired the Gipsy engine back into life. Ready to depart, no increase in power would budge the aircraft: she was stuck fast. I throttled back and yelled to the gathering of spectators, "Give me a shove!" In response to some enthusiastic shoulder power from the locals, the Magister started moving only to bog down again at the next sodden spot. My heart was in my mouth until I finally got a run on, spraying my willing assistants with mud. After a very hairy ground roll, and a little dodging, I pulled the stick back into my stomach and fed in a trickle of flap to eventually rise from the mire. Airborne and on my way to my new base, my flight eventually concluded at Cranage, home to 96 Squadron RAF.

CHAPTER SIX

Cat's Eyes

At Cranage the squadron motto reflected reality: 'We Prowl by Night'. 96 Squadron's reformation stemmed from the need for more night fighters to counter the ever increasing nightly blitz, particularly on the docks and factories of Liverpool. Armed with our trusty Hurricanes and doused in an all black paint scheme, we were designated as 'cat's eye' fighters to further emphasise the nocturnal role we were to play. The newer Hurricane Mk IIs packed a punch with four 20mm cannons projecting from their wings, while firepower for the Boulton Paul Defiant consisted of a gunner stationed in a rear 'ball turret'. My time with 96 Squadron was to prove one of the most dangerous postings I was to experience and the enemy only made up one aspect of the challenge.

To date I had a grand total of 434 hours experience, with a mere seventeen at night. I was classed as a 'fighter pilot-day', which meant the conditions that I had flown in at night were generally clear. A full moon was preferable and at least twelve miles visibility, though this was rare given the industrial refuse that filled the skies. My instrument flying experience was limited as well and had mainly taken place in my initial training, stuck under a canvas hood in a Hawker Hart by day. Telltale beams of sunlight would leak in through the cracks around the makeshift shroud to give one an idea of which way was up, but there were no such luxuries now. These were full blooded night operations in the worst of English weather.

Conditions were extremely hazardous for flying as the winter nights were characterised by low cloud mixed with the heavy pollutants from the industrial region. To worsen matters, the airfield was a grass field surrounded on all sides by 100-foot fir trees and only six miles from the lethal barrage balloons hovering over Crewe. It was very early days for night fighting and there was no manual for the conduct of operations. We were entering uncharted waters and the early techniques were far from successful. For all of the time, energy and manpower expended, we had minimal success.

One's vision at night was of paramount importance in these operations. When exposed to bright light, the pupils contract and subsequently take a prolonged period to dilate and adapt to darkness. With this in mind, there was an emphasis on the preservation of one's 'night vision' when flying cat's eye operations. As with so many of our good intentions, the execution let us down. Through the night we would eat from the bowls of carrots positioned around the mess and dispersal, while wearing sunglasses to protect our sight. When called to scramble we would no sooner have clambered into the cockpit than a flurry of torch beams would flash in your face as the airmen set about strapping you in. If this hadn't totally destroyed your night vision, the barrage of flames licking back from the Merlin's exhausts on starting up would be sure to do the trick.

Once airborne, the modus operandi involved the stacking of aircraft above the burning cities of England. This layering of aircraft was termed the 'Jacobs Ladder' and we would fly at levels above Angels 12 hopefully to remain out of the range of our own anti-aircraft batteries. Separated by a mere 500 feet, up to ten fighters would fly along pre-designated routes and look earthward for enemy bombers silhouetted against the glow of the overcast or the inferno of devastation below. Additionally, a spare pair of Hurricanes may be freed up to patrol at will, clear of the ladder. On the rare occasion that we managed to trap our foe, our dive to attack would often only serve to put us at the mercy of our own ack-ack as the bomber slipped away unscathed into the veil of darkness.

Where we should fly and at what levels was all predetermined at one of our radar installations. They could spot the inbound bombers well in advance and vector us to their position. For their part, the German bombers employed a 'blind' bombing system. This involved crossing a pair of beams generated by their ground stations with the point of intersection providing the queue to drop the bomb-load. Fortunately, our radar stations were able to 'bend' the beams and deceive the bombers into delivering their payload over the hills rather than the inhabited areas. To further complete the ruse, large fires were set in the wilderness to give the impression of a burning city. On a lighter note, the WD & HO Wills cigarette factory had caught fire during one raid and the aroma wafted across to Cranage. As an avid smoker in those days, one need only step outside and draw back to fill the lungs. Personally, I was a Lucky Strike smoker but the free prevailing wind was fine by me.

Returning to the airfield was also a challenge. Actually, it was more like a descent into hell. Given the proximity of the barrage balloons, an absence of radio communications from the ground, a tree-bordered airfield, no external aircraft lighting and always a minimum of fuel, it is a wonder that any of us ever made it down again.

Concealment of the airfield by night was obviously of the utmost importance. Consequently our initial guidance to the field was achieved by flying a bearing and distance from a beacon that was situated away from Cranage. We would be given these directions in our briefing and would write them clearly on our hands. Having flown the required heading, we would fix our position upwind over the field at around 1000 feet and buzz around like a swarm of low level insects. Using a Morse code key we would flash our aircraft identifier, a single letter, from a belly-mounted light. On seeing this light, the ground crew would signal you with a shielded green light to authorise an approach. Inherently the ground signaler was an inexperienced sergeant pilot or pilot officer. Understandably, these chaps were often rather twitchy about firing off their light into the night sky, thinking it an invitation to the Hun. With twelve, or so aircraft keen to get back on the deck you were fortunate if only one acknowledged the signal and started a descent into the confines of the approach. You could easily find yourself in company with unlit squadron mates who were just as desperate for terra firma. If this happened, you hoped the trusty 'flare-man' noticed and gave you a red light, in which case you both initiated a 'go-around' and attempted another approach.

There were two dull, blue glim lamps at either end of the field on which you lined up your landing. If you successfully cleared the fir trees, you then pumped the throttle to clear the last of the blinding sparks from the engine. Sitting about five knots above your stall speed with wheels and flaps lowered, holding 100 feet, you waited for the first glim lamp to slip by. As it disappeared under your port wingtip you counted to three, pushed the stick forward and then heaved it back in to your stomach. Accordingly the aircraft pitched nose down and then reared up in readiness to touch down. If you got it right, you made close to a three-point landing as desired. All that remained then was to keep the machine straight, gently squeeze on the brakes and re-orientate oneself with the airfield in order to park. Dismounting from your steed you would light up a cigarette or take a nervous piddle. Mind you, there was a maintenance order released forbidding urinating on the tailwheel. Apparently it could lead to corrosion!

My first operation was a night scramble at Cranage. Our thirty minutes notice dropped to fifteen and we knew there was something going on, so I geared up at dispersal and readied my aircraft. When the call finally came I taxied out and lined up on the runway only to be shocked by the very limited visibility ahead. My shock grew to horror when I realised that the overcast was sitting only a few hundred feet above the ground. I dropped my seat to its lowest possible setting and forced myself to focus on the instruments alone. Attempts at a visual departure in these conditions were fraught with danger and often resulted in fatalities shortly after becoming airborne.

I opened the throttle wide and the bright, blinding flames licked back from the exhaust ports. I danced lightly on the rudder pedals in an effort to keep straight and ever so gently eased the stick forward to raise the tail. The Hurricane was ready to fly, so trusting my limited instrument experience I raised the nose and climbed into the soup. Onwards and upwards I climbed through the void until, at 25,000 feet, I broke free into a brilliant moonlit night. It was beautiful smooth air with unlimited visibility and a floor beneath of snow white cloud. As I winged about the cloud tops I could be forgiven for thinking that I was weaving about icebergs surrounded by a vast arctic expanse. I patrolled the sky without seeing hide nor hair of the enemy, which only further added to the feeling that I was a world away from the war. It was with tremendous reluctance that I set myself to leave such serenity and descend back into the clag. With the help of the Ground Control Intercept (GCI) station, I popped out from the cloud base just above the field and landed without delay.

Whilst I returned safely from my first sortie, things didn't always go so smoothly. One particular evening, the standard recovery to land was not working well and they were forced to move the approach lamps five times due to the debris of crashed aircraft. Finally, out of space and low on aeroplanes, they closed the airfield to all operations. Such was the case for one Defiant as he attempted to land at Cranage. On approach he clipped the pine trees, wiping off his undercarriage and throwing his aircraft earthward. After impact, the aircraft rolled fully over, coming to rest the correct side up with no damage to the pilot. However, in the process of rolling over, the turret had been jammed down into the fuselage and prevented the gunner from freeing himself. With a hot engine and the smell of fuel vapours pervading the air, the somewhat apprehensive gunner began to call for assistance in no uncertain tone. The duty pilot, noting his dilemma with growing anxiety, rushed to the trapped gunner's aid. Attempting to smash the Perspex turret with the Verey pistol seemed to intensify the crewman's plight as he feared the distinct possibility of the flare gun launching an incendiary. After numerous blows, the duty pilot smashed through the turret, only to strike the otherwise uninjured gunner in the head and render him unconscious. Out of sympathy, the Defiant crew was given the next evening off from the perils of night fighting and chose to celebrate their escape royally at a local pub. As luck would have it, stepping off a two-inch kerb, the gunner tripped and broke his leg.

Rolling a Defiant on landing wasn't an everyday occurrence, though the machine was subject to many vices. With an absence of forward-facing firepower, they had been pulled from daylight operations where they had been on the receiving end of brutal punishment. Additionally, the weight of the turret ate into the performance margins of the aircraft and left it substantially underpowered, particularly in the climb. Even so, it had been chosen to supplement our Hurricanes in the cat's eye role and did go on to claim a level of success.

In achieving one of the squadron's victories, Alfred 'Scotty' Scott very nearly brought me down as well. A native of Nottingham, he was a volunteer reservist sergeant pilot and this night found him intercepting a Heinkel 111 bomber in his Defiant. His gunner was one of the best. A short, dark complexioned chap, he was lethally accurate with the four 7.69 mm machine guns that jutted from his turret. He had recently lost both parents in the bombing of London's east end and hated the Germans with unadulterated vehemence. Closing in from below, the gunner pounded the starboard engine and set it alight. He called to Scotty, "Move me across to port." He then proceeded to set the left engine on fire. By this time the bomber was doomed, but relentless, the gunner called again, "Drop back. I want to cover and see if anyone tries to bail out." Scotty later said he heard a series of bursts as his gunner made sure of the job. As this drama unfolded, I was climbing up through the murk and hadn't seen a thing. Just breaking through the cloud tops, my windscreen was filled with bomber, ablaze and plummeting to earth. Roaring past, the crippled bomber came very close to clobbering me out of the sky.

Scotty was a tremendous pilot and would go on to receive his commission and become a pilot officer. Returning to a Hurricane squadron, he was amongst eighty Hurricanes and Spitfires shot down in the raid on Dieppe in August 1942.

I wasn't always reliant on flaming Junkers to enjoy a near miss by night. One evening I was patrolling the line as briefed with my regular gunner, Sergeant Lazell, and as usual found a busy mind and constant lookout thwarted the cold's talons to some degree. Whilst the Jacob's Ladder hovered above its burning backdrop, we freelanced and awaited the call to steer us toward any inbound radar point. Still no word, we continued to peer into the gloom. Without warning, from the abyss roared a formation of Heinkel 111s. The camouflaged shadows flashed past with the associated din of a flock of radial engines. Narrowly missing numbers one and two, I emerged from the tail end of the group thankful that they hadn't adopted the British practice of tight formation. I wrenched the Defiant around in a split-arse turn to take chase, shuddering on the verge of the stall. Still banked steeply, I slipped down in an attempt to spot their glowing exhaust stacks from below. My gunner who had been at the ready was now compressed in his turret as the gravitational force pinned him down. I rolled out on the reciprocal of my previous heading, ready to engage... and then nothing. The formation had seemingly broken and made their way into the void from which they had emerged. My heart was still pounding in my chest as I searched in vain for any sign of the predators. They had gone and, once again, fate had been kind to me.

Vic Verity and I had shadowed each other somewhat through our RAF careers. From our training to our mid-channel meeting, we were now posted at the same cat's eye squadron. A true gentleman, Vic had come from a farming background in New Zealand. I recall one day as we drove around the English countryside that he paused and observed some livestock grazing. He was quiet and seemed almost melancholy as he surveyed the sheep going about their business. Seemingly paradoxical, it was often the case that the man needed in the cockpit was far removed from the man on the ground.

With the arrival of the Defiant, Vic had paired up with a gunner by the name of Sergeant Wake and together they made a formidable team, accounting for a number of the enemy. Whilst I was never a party to any of Vic's kills, we did travel together to seek out a Ju88 he had downed the previous night. On finding the wreckage, it was a messy sight. There were still bits of crew strewn about the wreck and a number of dogs helping themselves to the pickings. The home guard was probably too busy to trouble themselves with an enemy crash site. Nevertheless, like my evacuation from Dunkirk, it was a graphic reminder of what war was all about. Vic Verity would go on to see action in the Middle East and the Mediterranean, earning the DFC and becoming an ace in the process. At the war's end he returned to the life he loved, farming in New Zealand.

Chaps like Verity and Scotty were tremendous comrades and another character from 96 Squadron was Harold 'Knocker' North. He carried a bullet in his chest, precariously close to his heart. He had claimed a kill earlier in the war, but had also received a lead memento that the surgeons were unable to remove. It certainly didn't seem to affect his performance, though he soon lost his interest in the cat's eye operations. Another New Zealander, he was a skilful aerobatic pilot and was able to wring the absolute maximum out of a Hurricane, however, the Defiant was a very different matter. Underpowered and relatively staid, 'Knocker' didn't enjoy flying the Defiant; not many of us did for that matter. In combination with all weather night-fighting, he had enough of the show and sought out the New Zealand network. In very un-Royal Air Force style, the Kiwis were able to move between squadrons via a very efficient system. Totally unsanctioned by Command, they would make contact with brethren from the homeland and organise transfers between units. I congratulate them on their initiative and under this 'scheme' Knocker was able to bid 96 Squadron farewell. However, his luck didn't hold and he subsequently failed to return from a sortie over France, despite the fact that his squadron never encountered enemy fighters. With the German gunners always ready to greet you, one couldn't help but wonder whether Knocker's embedded bullet had finally found its mark.

In contrast, my time at 96 Squadron was in many ways about survival. Despite the best that the weather, the night, the enemy and fate could dish out to me, I still managed to be there at the end of the day. Death surrounded us and could make its presence known in any number of ways. For my part, the nine months at Cranage saw me grow up at a speed beyond my years and in many ways, laid the foundation for my survival through the rest of the war.

*   *   *

Cranage was predominantly about night fighting in the worst of weather, but the posting also saw many and varied 'alternate operations' take place. Some of these were humorous, whilst others were simply terrifying. Each of the experiences was unique and added to the tapestry that was a fighter pilot's life. Along the way, I even found time to fall in love and get married.

One of the more amusing tales of my time with 96 Squadron, involved a local police sergeant with whom I became friends after originally running foul of the law. My old green Renault had a slight problem with the brakes in that they didn't really work. This had led me to dribbling through a stop sign and incurring the wrath of an officer of the law, who subsequently charged me. I was rather dirty about this, here I was putting my neck on the line for king and country night after night and this miserable 'blue bottle' had stung me with a ticket. My time would come though. Another offence at the time was the failure to immobilise one's vehicle as per the anti-invasion instructions which was normally achieved by removing the rotor from the car's engine. I was fortunate enough to spot two police vehicles on a liaison visit to the squadron which had been parked and left without being immobilised. I took it upon myself to comply with instructions and made off with the rotors and henceforth went flying. Returning from my sortie I found the policemen in disarray and sweating about what they would tell the superintendent. I dawdled passed this scene, nonchalantly tossing the rotors from hand to hand. I confided my sad tale of the stop sign to the sergeant in charge and it was agreed that the rotors would be a fair trade for the 'correction' of my transgression. From that point Sergeant Hamlet and I became good friends.

I was scheduled for a test flight in a Defiant around dusk one evening and sought out Sergeant Hamlet to see if he would like to ride in the turret for the flight. A brief hop, up and down. He leapt at the opportunity. We were chatting over the interphone when searchlights started to comb the sky and a display of fireworks lit up from below. It was a German air raid and I was effectively defenceless with a civilian sitting in my gun turret who was unable to work the guns. With flak bursts erupting all around, I kept one eye out for escorting fighters and made speed for Cranage as the war began to escalate around us. Whilst I realised the severity of the situation, my friend thought it was absolutely amazing and was fascinated by the show being presented for him. My only thought was getting back on the ground and it was with true appreciation that I felt the blades of English grass kiss my tyres.

The Renault that had let me down at the stop sign did prove useful nevertheless. It had led to my introduction to Sergeant Hamlet and, more importantly, served as transport in my ground-based pursuit of one Doreen Wilson. The London girl who would become my wife.

Doreen recalls:

> I had left school at seventeen after passing my London University matriculation exam with distinctions in German and English but as my widowed mother could not afford to send me to university I had to get a job. This turned out to be very good as in 1937 I was given a job with ICI (Imperial Chemical Industries) as the personal assistant to the chief standards engineer. The office was at Millbank, a very swish new building near the Houses of Parliament at Westminster.
>
> In 1939, prior to the outbreak of war, all head office personnel were either sacked or dispersed to various ICI establishments around the country. My department was sent to Northwich in Cheshire and there I shared a flat with two girlfriends, Freda Turner and Hilda Palmer. This flat was upstairs to a

dentist's surgery and conveniently situated between the local fire and bus stations in central Northwich. As three young, unattached girls from London you can imagine we had many friends; local scientists from ICI and many servicemen in those days. They were all very polite and good company with no sex involved. We played records on our wind up gramophone and sat around drinking coffee with occasional visits to the cinema or local pubs.

One evening my girlfriend, Freda, had a date with a Scottish air gunner, Johnnie Ritchie and I with a gorgeous Czech pilot. We were awaiting the knock on our door, when we opened it to my surprise and disappointment there was no dashing Bill Vesely but another person, a pilot in a very scruffy uniform with long hair. My immediate reaction was that I didn't wish to be seen out and about with such a person as I had a very high standard and reputation, so I suggested that we all went to the cinema so as not to be seen. However, this chap everybody called 'Mac' turned out to be a very nice quiet sort and he told me later that he had decided there and then that I was the one for him! The next evening, uninvited, he was on the doorstep again. I had other dates to keep when he announced that he was going to haunt me! I took all this with a pinch of salt, but sure enough he turned up every evening before night flying. He would just stay for a few minutes and then go on his way. He was flying Hurricanes and Defiants with 96 Squadron at Cranage and often he would fly really low between the fire station and the flat, terrorising the neighbourhood. At this time Mac owned a bright green Renault car, which unfortunately had no brakes. As a consequence, after we had been out for the evening, and he was delivering me back to the flat, he had to slow down and I would fling open the door and jump out. It was not the most romantic way to end an evening. One thing led to another and I eventually realised what a sincere and genuine person Mac was. I was twenty-one and Mac was twenty when he took me to Glasgow to meet his parents and family. We had a

picnic by Loch Lomond and Mac wore his kilt, he
had great legs for a kilt! About this time Mac
inherited £200 from an old aunt so was able to buy
a better car, a very small Ford. The old Renault was
abandoned on the airfield and became a gun
emplacement in due course. Mac also bought me an
engagement ring, a beautiful ruby with diamond
shoulders set in platinum and costing all of £40. So
three months after meeting it seems we were
engaged, full marks to Mac's perseverance and
dedication.

Aside from courting, perseverance and dedication were
worthwhile traits for a pilot being asked to undertake all
manner of tasks. At one stage I was given the job of flying a
Westland Lysander along various patrol lines to give the anti-
aircraft batteries practice at sighting a target with the assistance
of newly implemented radar. I had never flown a Lysander
before, but in the now familiar style, I was sent on my way to
learn as I went. With its high gull wing and huge 'spatted' fixed
undercarriage, it was built for purpose not speed and as an
army co-operation aircraft it was destined to fly numerous
clandestine missions for the French Resistance behind enemy
lines. There was nothing secretive about my task and I sincerely
hoped that the gun crews didn't have anything up the spout.
With leading edge flaps, I was all but hovering, waiting for
them to line me up.

For a period, the squadron CO at 96 was a chap by the name
of Bobby Burns. A good-natured Rhodesian, he was well liked
by his men. One evening the weather was so foul that we were
all stood down; completely off readiness. The CO issued an
invitation, "Let's go lads. We're off to the pub," so we made
our way to Holmes Chapel and a favoured hotel that always let
us drink well after time. We were making the most of the
evening when the phone rang and the CO was summoned,
"Things are stirring. Make your way back to base." On our
return we were ordered into the air and the CO looked around
for his experienced pilots, taking into account the last few
hours of rest and relaxation. I was one of the number and
found myself, once again, spearing into filthiest of weather, and
wondering what in heaven's name I was doing there. Having
consumed a sizeable amount of English ale, my dilemma was

compounded by an ever-increasing urge to pee. It was highly distracting, but I was committed to not using the relief tube provided for such instances. A pet fear of mine was to be jumped by the enemy whilst in the midst of urinating and this wasn't going to be the night I broke my rule. I managed to hold on, just, and the scramble turned out to be a phoney call once again. We joked that ops knew our predicament and were having a lend of us. The experience frightened the hell out of me and it was probably only later that I fully realised how very fortunate we were not to lose an aircraft considering our state.

To keep our aircraft flying and vessels afloat, the nation's resources were heavily burdened and the war effort took many forms in the pursuit of funds and materials. There would be 'drives' to collect all styles of metal to go into the manufacture of the war machine. People would turn up with iron gates, pots, pans and anything else you could imagine that was able to be melted down. There were also 'Spitfire Days' where towns would raise funds in order to sponsor the construction of the elliptical-winged fighter. In return for the generous support on the home front, we were called upon to 'fly the flag' by performing impromptu air displays; or more accurately, beat up the city at low level. This may be done in vic formation, or in line astern where one after the other we would lift the roof tiles. Strangely, given my combat experience, these beat ups were the source of a recurring nightmare for me. I would dream that I was tearing along the streets of Manchester when I realised that I had tram tracks running above me. I could not imagine how I was going to get out of this spot, boxed in and unable to climb. My stress would grow and grow when a town square would appear ahead. Contrary to the reality of a fighter's turning radius, I was able to reverse my direction and escape. This dream haunted me time and again.

Just before my term at Cranage drew to a close, we were visited by one of my old aircraft from Hullavington, an Audax with a small glider in tow. The purpose of the exercise was to give us fighter pilots experience in attacking a small, manoeuvrable glider with a vastly different airspeed to ourselves. It was envisioned that gliders may well be used by the Germans in an invasion, just as was the case with the Allies years later. One after the other we would roll our Hurricanes and Defiants in on the target in mock attacks. Back on the ground I was kindly offered to gain another perspective on the exercise in the two-seat glider. Considering myself fortunate to be asked, I leapt at the opportunity and was soon 'in tow' behind the Audax. It turned out to be an absolutely terrifying experience. Staring down the jaws of the attacking fighters, I sat there totally defenceless as one after the other, my squadron mates roared down at me. From the glider's silent cockpit, the Merlin's scream was deafening as the fighters missed by a minimal distance. I could do nothing but wait until the assault was over and recover my heart from my mouth.

The war was not always about a clash of eagles. Often it was just a case of doing the simple things right and learning on the job. You had a pair of wings proudly displayed on your best blue uniform and your senior officers made sure you continued to earn them by thrusting you into all sorts of predicaments. Training was always minimal. Whilst the state of the war stole from us the luxury of time, the most predominant factor was that we were often doing things for the *first* time. Night-fighting was a new concept and we were subject to all manner of trials, like lab rats in the cockpit. Some survived while others didn't. If you didn't keep your wits about you, those wings on your chest could all too easily become wings on your back.

CHAPTER SEVEN

60 Operational Training Unit

My arrival at 60 Operational Training Unit was, personally, somewhat disappointing. I had just been promoted to flight lieutenant and felt I was strong on survival but weak on 'gong collecting'. Chaps weren't known for receiving the DFC doing circuits and bumps. It was wartime and I had managed to outlive the rigours of being shot down and flying cat's eye operations only to slide down into a training role. Scotty's arrival from 96 Squadron lifted my spirits a little and we both set about instructing, though not officially rated as flight instructors.

Our home was RAF East Fortune, a tuberculosis hospital in its former life and not ideally suited in the present as a training airfield. Situated at East Lothian, south of Edinburgh, it was susceptible to the miserable weather that drifted in from the coast in time for night training. Furthermore, there was a large hill with the look of an extinct volcano adjacent to the runway. Named Berwick Law, this knoll took a steady toll on our pupils. To such surrounds I flew all matter of machinery. My old friends, the Magister, Defiant and Blenheim and some new acquaintances, the Miles Master, Airspeed Oxford and the high performance Bristol Beaufighter.

As an OTU our trainees were graduates of flight training schools and arrived into our hands with their new wings proudly displayed above the breast pocket. Our task was to convert them onto the various new types and make them wise to the operational world. A substantial slice of our training was at night and amongst our sorties we also trialled a new lighting system that utilised sodium. Just as at Cranage, there was always some form of experimentation taking place in the field of night ops and this latest unsuccessful venture had a blinding effect. Away from the cockpit there was no ground school of note and most of their education came from our combined experiences at operational squadrons. I flew a large amount of time in the Miles Master, which served as a lead-in aircraft for those pilots destined for Hurricanes and Spitfires. A manoeuvrable little two-seater, it was armed with a single fixed Browning machine gun and the ability to carry eight practice bombs allowing us to train our new chums in the various aspects of combat flying.

The Bristol Beaufighter was a wonderful aircraft with an underlying fault in the early models. In the event of an engine failure, you were frequently unable to fully 'feather', or stop the propeller on the failed engine. This leads to a state of asymmetry as one engine powers forward to keep you afloat, whilst the other windmills and drags the other side back. This imbalance causes tremendous problems in terms of controllability and continued flight and had claimed a number of victims in a relatively short time. My first experience on the Beaufighter occurred in June 1942 and was rather eventful in a totally different way. The aircraft was equipped with a ladder under the nose by which access to the cockpit was achieved. It came down through a hatch, which was subsequently closed and secured for flight. On this occasion, the erks had failed to secure the hatch fully after I'd climbed aboard and, as a result, it dropped open as I returned to land. When it opened it was like an air brake. My airspeed decayed rapidly and approached the dreaded stall, at which point I would have very little say in any continued flight. Unaware of what was amiss, I opened up the throttles in search of power and speed. The two Merlins slowly responded to give me sufficient thrust to just remain aloft. I dragged the Beaufighter over the fence and landed it without further drama.

Our CO at East Fortune was Wing Commander Oliver. While students prepared for their night training, the CO would take flight each evening around dusk to observe the weather moving in from the nearby North Sea. On his return he would do a low level, slow roll along the flarepath. One evening the stunt didn't come off and he lost height as he rolled the aircraft inverted. Without height to spare, he scraped his head off in his final ill-judged aerobatic display.

Funnily enough, Wing Commander Oliver was equally known amongst the troops for his dog, an absolutely huge Saint

Bernard, which would frequently visit the entrance of the mess where his master was drinking at the bar. This massive dog would subsequently set about shagging all the greatcoats as they hung on the rack. His efforts to reproduce himself were totally unsuccessful and left us with a rather unwanted mess.

The lifestyle was very relaxed and the operation was at times downright boring. Away from the idleness of my duties, Doreen and I set about getting married and escaping on our honeymoon. She recounts:

> Our marriage was arranged for January 10th 1942. That was six months after our first meeting and what a party our wedding was! The guests were my colleagues from ICI and most of 96 Squadron, my mother and two of my sisters came up from London and Mac's mother came down from Glasgow. The church was very small and was filled to capacity, it was a thirteenth century half timbered building and the unusual thing was that it stood in the same grounds as the very old pub called 'The Bells of Peover' (pronounced Peever) where we held the party. We spent our first night at the Midland Hotel in Manchester where there was an air raid alarm in the middle of the night and everyone had to vacate their rooms and stand in the corridor! We travelled by train the next morning to Edinburgh. All the compartments were packed and so were the corridors for the ten-hour journey to Scotland. We spent our short honeymoon at a small place near Edinburgh called Peebles. The hotel, 'The Black Barony', was like an ancient castle set in the most beautiful grounds. On our arrival it snowed heavily and no one could get in or out for a few days which suited us fine. Our room was called the King's Room. It had a huge four-poster bed, thick velvet curtains and an enormous open log fire and there was a little secret door to a staircase used by the maid who brought our breakfast. We took a few walks in the snow but it was very cold while our room was so cosy.

Regretfully, my leave couldn't last forever, so it was back to

RAF East Fortune where I again took up residence in the less than luxurious mess. Doreen joined me in Scotland a short time later and we found digs in a stuffy boarding house at North Berwick. The two old ladies who ran the place were very unsympathetic to our late nights and drinking, which seemed to happen frequently. Incidentally, Doreen had changed her previous expensive taste in drinks from Rye highballs to brown ale. This was in keeping with our RAF financial restrictions, as I was earning the lordly sum of thirteen shillings and sixpence per day as a flight lieutenant. Doreen used to fill in time by helping at the soldiers canteen several days a week; officers' wives were expected to do voluntary war work. Meanwhile, I continued to instruct and instruct.

Despite keeping the Beaufighter in one piece and the various other close calls one experiences with student pilots, it was at OTU that I came close to ending my air force career. I was informed by Lloyds Bank that my cheque to the boarding house had not been honoured as my account was now overdrawn. Our pay was regularly behind schedule and I had inadvertently bounced a cheque. The grand sum was less than a pound. At the time, a bounced cheque was an offence subject to court martial and the matter was most serious. I quickly organised amends, though the landlords were not terribly understanding. Perhaps those late nights had finally taken their toll. In any case, when the cheque finally cleared we left with due haste, leaving behind my brand new plum pyjamas in the rush. So red-faced was I over the incident that I never returned to collect the sleepwear.

Such matters seemed to be the height of action for me at OTU, though my idle days were rapidly drawing to a close. Whilst I readied myself for a new posting, Doreen readied for the birth of our first child. The war in the air served as one aspect of the conflict, though life in everyday Britain for the civilian population was also coloured by sacrifice and loss. Doreen lived that life at close quarters:

> Food rationing was in full swing, we had ration
> books, allocating minute amounts of butter, meat
> and sugar with other coupons for all canned goods,
> materials and clothes. At the time of our wedding I
> couldn't spare coupons to buy a white dress to be
> worn for just a few hours so I had bought a rather

nice two piece suit in maroon with velvet collar and pockets and which I was able to wear for years after. Now that I was pregnant I was given a special green ration book for slightly more rations. The best thing was that the holder of a green ration book was allowed to go to the head of any queue and there were plenty of queues in those days.

The blackout was horrendous, every single window had to have black opaque curtains or blinds and not a chink of light must be seen. Air Raid Precaution (ARP) wardens patrolled after dark to check the blackout was complete. Car headlights too had to be covered by a black metal hood with louvres to throw the dim light downwards with the result that you couldn't see anything. Once in a thick fog, a real peasouper, I had to get out and walk in front with a very dim torch!

Our next surprise was that I had become pregnant with our first daughter Jane so I returned to the flat in Northwich to await Mac's next posting which was in July 1942 to 87 Squadron at Charmy Down near Bath. Mac set off from Scotland on the long trip south in our little Ford and picked me up on the way. It was a long trip and we got as far as Chipping Sodbury which was close to our destination but we were both exhausted. We tried for a bed at a well known pub which was full but, as it was so late at night and we were pretty desperate, the landlady kindly put up a very narrow folding bed in what seemed to be a large cupboard and we both squeezed onto it, just grateful to get our heads down. Charmy Down was a sort of small add-on to RAF Colerne close by. The mess was a lovely small country house with a tame jackdaw which used to steal anything shiny left lying about, people lost shirt studs and cuff links – these things were still in normal everyday use as pilots flew in full uniform with stiff collars and black ties. After the initial grant of £50 on commissioning, any uniform purchases were at one's own expense. There was a very good supplier called Gieves in Bond Street in London and they would accept monthly payments and, if a pilot was killed, they would write off any debts.

We were now established at my new posting with Doreen living nearby. East Fortune had been a period of relative inactivity for me and I was now seemingly to be thrust back into the dark world of night operations. What I did not foresee was our return to France within the month and a daylight mission that would go down in history for the decimation of over 100 RAF fighters.

CHAPTER EIGHT

Disaster at Dieppe

My new commanding officer at 87 Squadron was Squadron Leader 'Splinters' Smallwood. In time he would become Chief of Air Staff, but for now he commanded a 'Turbinlite' Squadron out of RAF Colerne. Turbinlite was a new night-fighting tactic that involved Hurricanes flying in company with searchlight-equipped bombers. I would have greater involvement with this form of warfare at a later date, but my immediate call to arms was very different.

I had arrived at the squadron as a supernumerary pilot. A relatively experienced flight lieutenant, I was as unsure of my new role as the squadron was of how best to utilise me. My initial missions were night operations where I would fly the Hurricane as a 'stooge' for the ground-based searchlight crews to get a bead on me. It was an eerie feeling going from absolute darkness into the eruption of brilliant light and like so many of the co-operative exercises, you were hoping that all parties were aware that this was only an exercise. I was just learning the ropes at 87 when something began to stir. We were moved across to RAF Tangmere and it seemed obvious that this wasn't a night-fighting based move.

Unbeknown to us, vessels had set sail in darkness the previous evening to land troops at Dieppe on the French coast. When the morning of August 19th dawned, things were already going terribly wrong. Whilst we weren't privy to the exact details, we were told that our troops, mainly Canadians, were hung up and couldn't get past the centre of the city. We were instructed that our role would be one purely of air to ground attack against the heavily fortified coastline. Specifically the western headland, which was code-named 'Hindenburg'. Anchored off the coast was a British naval vessel with whom

Top left: A young Kenneth McGlashan prior to the outbreak of war in 1939.

Top right: Ground crew at Leconfield take some time out for a lighter moment.

Bottom: A Miles Magister of 245 Squadron in flight.

Top: 245 Squadron pilots, Marsland, Hammond and McGlashan (left to right), take a stroll near Leconfield.

Bottom: Believed to be the only photo of R-DX taken in its short operational life. This belief is supported by the 'R' on the wheel chock and the top of an 'R' just visible on its port side.

Top: June 2nd 1940. Two days after being shot down over Dunkirk, McGlashan (seated far left) is photographed at Hawkinge with 245 Squadron. (Note the oil stains on his trouser legs.)

Bottom: Robert 'Pengy' West proudly poses with his Hawker Hurricane Mk 1 before being lost over France in June 1940.

Top: The loyal ground crew that awaited the return of R-DX from its ill-fated sortie over Dunkirk.

Bottom: Alan Treanor. Along with 'Pengy' West, Treanor failed to return from France on June 1st, 1940.

Opposite page: Ken McGlashan and Geoff Howitt relax on a bridge near Leconfield. The two pilots were also in company the day McGlashan was shot down over Dunkirk.

Top: 245 Squadron Hawkinge 1940. McGlashan at rear, second from end on the right and Squadron Leader Eric Whitley is seated at centre in the middle row.

Bottom: Waiting. Dawn readiness at Hawkinge 1940.

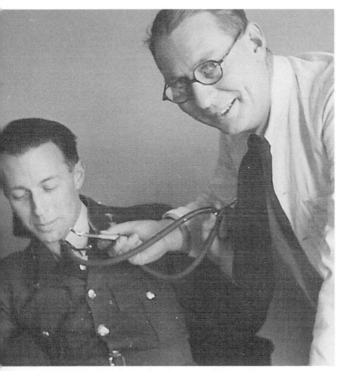

Top: A native of New Zealand, 'Ginge' Mowat and an earlier form of communication at Hawkinge.

Bottom left: Tables turned. A medical officer at Hawkinge has seemingly become the patient.

Bottom right: Pilot Officer Marsland during 245 Squadron's term at Aldergrove.

Top: A ground staff sergeant joins the pilots of B Flight 245 Squadron at Aldergrove for an informal portrait.

Middle: Pilot Officer Pennington atop the wing of Hurricane S-DX at Aldergrove.

Bottom: Pennington (left) makes his thoughts known while McConnell looks on. (245 Squadron Aldergrove)

Top: A native of Ireland, Pilot Officer McConnell with a Hawker Hurricane at Aldergrove.

Bottom: The men who kept them flying. Ground crew at Aldergrove are joined by a sergeant pilot.

Top: On the hardstand. A Hawker Hurricane at the ready following maintenance.

Middle: A formal studio portrait of a young Kenneth McGlashan taken in 1941.

Bottom left: Wedding bells. Kenneth and Doreen McGlashan leave the church on January 10th, 1942 to begin their journey together.

Bottom right: 96 Squadron mate, Vic Verity with Doreen McGlashan at Cranage (circa 1942).

Top left: Seconded to fly with BOAC out of Cairo in 1944, this passport-style shot captures Kenneth in his time abroad.

Top right: A tremendous marksman, Kenneth holds a trophy from a 'meet' at Bisley in 1947.

Bottom: Top marks. Competitors stand by the 'Fighter Command' leader board at a Bisley shoot. A winning Kenneth McGlashan is third from right.

Top left: The CO in mess kit. Squadron Leader McGlashan in his time at the helm of 25 Squadron RAF (circa 1949-50).

Top right: VIP tour. Kenneth shows Miss New Zealand the business end of a de Havilland Mosquito in 1950.

Bottom: 25 Squadron victorious. A formal portrait of Kenneth McGlashan and his squadron following their success at the Air Firing competition at Acklington in 1949.

Top: A short reprieve. Kenneth and course-mates enjoy a break from staff college at Bracknell as they gather on the deck of *HMS Illustrious*.

Bottom: The silverware. More victories at Bisley for Kenneth and his team-mates. McGlashan is standing centre at rear.

Top: Phoenix rising. Hurricane RD-X sees the light of day after nearly half a century as it is carefully recovered from the Dunkirk sand.

Bottom left: A poignant reminder. The pictured memorial to the Dunkirk evacuation is sited on the location of the Mole where Kenneth boarded *The Golden Eagle*.

Bottom right: Battle of Britain day 2002, Sydney, Australia.

Top left: Kenneth McGlashan enjoying a well-earned retirement at his Australian home.

Top right: Sixty wonderful years. Kenneth and Doreen celebrate their wedding anniversary in 2002.

Middle: Treasured memories. An array of Kenneth's wartime belongings, including dog tags, are laid out on his RAF logbook, opened to the month of May 1940.
(Owen Zupp)

Bottom: A contemporary shot of Kenneth's uniform coat and decorations. Still preserved in immaculate condition.
(Owen Zupp)

Top: Standing tall. Photographed in late 2005, R-DX is well on its way to taking to the air once again.

Middle: Stepping back in time. Kenneth boards a light aircraft to once again fly over the beaches of Dunkirk.

Bottom: Reunited. Kenneth meets R-DX once again after more than fifty years.

we would check in to confirm that our briefing still stood. I was to lead the rear section, just as I had on my eventful mission to Dunkirk two years before.

Whilst 87 Squadron had a number of punchy, cannon-equipped Hurricane Mk IIs, I was allocated an old trusty Mk I with its eight Brownings. Such was the lot of a newly arrived supernumerary pilot. I was to take part in the second sortie across the Channel after our first wave returned from its dawn hop. Strapped in, the engine primed, I kicked the Merlin into life. The blades ahead flicked over at an ever increasing rate to form the now familiar disc, throwing airflow back past my open canopy. Chocks away and I was bound for France once again.

The crossing of the Channel was uneventful but as Dieppe loomed ahead, the ferocity of the artillery barrage was evident. We contacted the control vessel to confirm that our target was the same as briefed, to which we received a very scratchy confirmation. The CO was flying lower and lower with the resultant loss of radio range and quality. As we neared the controller we came under fire from British naval anti-aircraft gunners who took all single-engined fighters to be Me109s. With an air-filled *VOOF* my mission nearly ended there and then as a friendly shell passed close enough to be heard.

The sky was absolutely thick with the black smoke of exploding shells. The cliff tops were littered with houses within which were stationed light German anti-aircraft guns. Their fire was terribly accurate and in company with the barrage from their heavy guns, there was little room left in the sky for us. All the while, the squadron leader flew lower and lower to the extent that we at the rear were rapidly running out of air. Still locked in rigid formation, our leader seemed oblivious to the predicament of those behind him as the water loomed below and the cliff tops stood above us. All the while the German fire was being supplemented by a rain of empty shell cases and bombs from aircraft above. Crossing the coast, land and sea came too close for comfort. I broke away and my numbers two and three fanned out. From that point I was on my own.

I pulled the Hurricane over the tiles of the hostile roof tops and headed inland. I couldn't actually believe that I had made it across the coast without being hit by some form of flying metal. As I roared across the French countryside, I saw a gathering of German soldiery ahead in a field they shared with some livestock. They moved to take cover, though a lone soldier with a light machine gun set his weapon on its pole and pointed it in my direction. My guns were already set to fire, so I dropped my nose and gave a squirt. My shots landed upon him and, unfortunately, an innocent French cow. As that scene swept below my belly, our briefed target suddenly appeared ahead, positioned on a small hill.

The gun emplacement was of a serious size and surrounded by a parapet, below which the gun crews took cover as I approached. There was no sign of my squadron and I could only assume that they had been and gone. It was obvious that my .303s weren't going to have any impact on the walls surrounding the position, so I assessed my best way to get a crack at the personnel. I was aware that the gun crews would dive for their sand-bagged walls at the first sight of me, so I undertook to introduce an element of surprise by attacking from different approaches. At treetop height I skirted a valley before turning back towards the target. I stayed as low as possible for as long as possible before popping up and taking aim. I fired off a burst as the crews dived in all directions and then roared over their heads. Swinging away, I set myself again from a different perspective. Again, heads up, a brief glimpse and fire.

I made three attacks and was setting myself for a fourth when there was a series of chest wrenching bangs. These were accompanied by huge columns of earth being hurled skyward and I looked up to see a bunch of our 'Hurri-bombers' releasing their payload of 250 pounders. I was down in the dirt, the wall of the gun's parapet lay ahead at eye height and I readied for one last pass when all hell broke loose. A deafening explosion erupted directly below me and threw my Hurricane hundreds of feet into the air. The percussion and negative 'g' force starved my Merlin's carburettor of fuel causing all to go quiet up front. I was seemingly hanging in mid-air with a choking engine, for a few of those seconds that seem to take forever, I thought I'd had it.

Thankfully, my engine burst back into life and my heart recommenced beating. The Hurri-bombers had obviously had enough of me mucking about with the target and I tended to agree. I dropped everything and got out of there as fast as I could. I crossed the coast back through the flak and headed for

England, only to notice that my engine was now rapidly starting to overheat. The explosion had obviously thrown all manner of debris into my radiator and the Merlin was starting to cook. My return across the Channel was nerve wracking as I attempted to nurse the crippled engine over the expanse of water. Finally I crossed the coast and limped into Tangmere.

Pilots milled around the intelligence officer recounting their experiences from Operation Jubilee. I stood amongst them awaiting my turn to debrief when my fitter approached and beckoned me towards my battered Hurricane. I left the queue and wandered over to where the erk was crouched on his haunches beside the Hawker's belly. "Look at this", he said disbelievingly as he flexed the underside centre section with his hand. The bottom of my aircraft was pulp. In the sagging canvas hung wires, pipes and numerous other pieces of the Hurricane's anatomy, literally hanging by a thread. I was aghast. The gods of the French coast had favoured me once again.

Back at debriefing, pilots were readying for another wave of sorties. With my Hurricane out of commission, I wasn't going anywhere. Looking back, my close call that morning probably saved my neck as things hotted up on the subsequent missions to Dieppe. Our briefing early that morning had us attack perpendicular to the coastline, cross over and proceed inland to the target. At some point after my sortie, the tactics changed to have the Hurricanes fly parallel to the coastline. This was absolute suicide. With the mass of firepower lining the cliff tops, the Hurricanes would be passing by like tin ducks in a shooting gallery. Combined with the Luftwaffe, there was a myriad of means to be felled at Dieppe that day.

For those of us earthbound at Tangmere, a light sea fog had rolled in that afternoon. It prevented further sorties and, in doing so, may well have saved many lives. With flying abandoned for the day, we retired to the mess for a beer or two. As we stood around counting heads and comparing stories, the hum of conversation was broken by the howl of an approaching fighter at high speed. A sole Me 109 was attempting to line up the field for a hit and run raid with its lone bomb. He obviously couldn't get a good fix on the field through the low-lying mist and released his ordinance some distance away where it fell harmlessly. We returned to the bar, conscious that a number of our chaps would not be enjoying a beer tonight.

The RAF lost over 100 aircraft that day, with a large proportion being Hurricanes. It was the greatest allied air loss in a single day of the entire war. The majority was lost to anti-aircraft fire as opposed to air-to-air combat and many of the aircraft that did return were in a state similar to my aircraft. Having seen the wall of flak that met us, it was not at all surprising. From my perspective, the Germans were well prepared to defend the ground and the air. We seemed to lack any element of surprise and then worsened our cause by dawdling along in front of their guns. Despite the Allied propaganda, the operation was an unmitigated failure with heavy losses sustained by all involved, particularly the Canadians. On a personal note, my good friend Scotty was lost in his Hurricane that day. We had flown cat's eye and at OTU together, though when I made my way to 87, Scotty went to my old unit, 245 Squadron. His loss was yet another instance of the reality of war; that good men die far too young.

Within weeks of Dieppe I was on my way again. No longer a homeless supernumerary, I had been given posting to 536 Squadron at Fairwood Common in South Wales. Like 87 Squadron, it was involved in night fighting Turbinlite operations and like 96 Squadron cat's eye ops, it was highly ineffective.

CHAPTER NINE

Turbinlite Tango

It is hard to imagine a form of night fighting that was less efficient than our Jacob's Ladders at Cranage. Even so, Turbinlite operations would have to go close to wrenching the hard earned mantle from those stacks of Hurricanes, hovering above a burning Merseyside. In concept it may have made sense to a desk-bound staff committee, but in execution it was an absolute nightmare, fraught with danger. Yet here I was again in the midst of another great nocturnal experiment.

As with many 'specialist' squadrons of the day, their origins lay with a smaller 'flight' that was subsequently upgraded to a higher status and 536 Squadron was no exception. Evolving from 1457 Flight, we were based at Fairwood Common and equipped with American-built Havocs alongside our Mk II Hurricanes. Operating in an integrated fashion, the intention was to provide a lethal 'hunter-killer' combination against raiding bombers.

The twin-engined Havocs served as the hunters and were fitted with a colossal 2,700 million candle-power searchlight, or 'Turbinlite' if referred to by its trade name. This man-made sun illuminated the target for the hunter and was powered by two tons of batteries which were crammed into the bomb bay. Further weighed down with Airborne Interception (AI) radar, this stockpile of equipment meant that there was no performance remaining to carry any offensive weaponry. Crewed by a pilot and navigator/radar operator, the Havoc was gradually replaced by a later model which came to be known as the Boston.

Within days of arriving at the squadron I was endorsed on the Havoc via the standard RAF 'laissé faire' procedure of "read the handling notes and off you go son". Whilst I flew a

few hops involving airborne interceptions and radio tests in the
hunter, my role again lay with the Hurricane as the killer
component of the partnership. Originally it was conceived that
a pair of Hurricanes would fly in close formation either side of
the Havoc, though in practice this proved to be sheer murder.
The combination was reduced to an unarmed Havoc flying
with a sole Hurricane which alone carried the firepower to
bring down the enemy bomber.

From the first moment, Turbinlite operations were
dangerous. On being scrambled we were to form up on the
Havoc, which was no mean feat given a significant difference in
speed between the aircraft and the fact that these were night
operations. To choreograph this pairing, the Hurricane would
take off first with the Turbinlite becoming airborne immediately thereafter. Once airborne, we would set the Hurricane
in a climbing left turn until we were flying a reciprocal heading
and parallel to the runway. Struggling to sight and then
orientate with the Turbinlite's navigation lights, we would
judge when he was climbing out and execute another 180
degree turn, though this time diving towards our hunter. When
at close quarters, we would join up on the starboard side of the
Turbinlite and tuck in as tightly as possible. Both aircraft would
then extinguish their navigation lights and be consumed by the
night's envelope of darkness.

As success of the operation was dependant upon stealth,
both the hunters and killers bore an all black paint scheme.
With the nav lights off, the only remaining illumination was the
Turbinlite's minimal station-keeping lights. Situated on the
upper and lower surfaces of the wings and close to the fuselage,
these small aft-facing spotlights were aimed along painted
white stripes. These strips of light were one's sole reference for
formation flying and could prove disorientating at the best of
times. Flying through cloud rendered the white stripes and
spotlights nearly invisible and placed crews of the Hurricanes
and Havocs in very real danger of collision.

Climbing out, the formation would be steered to intercept
the target by ground radar until the Havoc's airborne radar
picked up the intruder. From that point our hunter would lead
us to the target and we would set about an 'attack drill'. This
drill involved closing to minimum range on the enemy at which
time the Havoc would advise us that we were getting "warm".
On this call the Hurricane pilot would note the compass

heading and immediately fast climb to 500 feet above the Havoc, all the while endeavouring to keep his 'radar mate' in sight. If the interception was proceeding well, the Havoc would call "Boil!" and switch on his blinding Turbinlite, illuminating the hapless foe. On this cue the Hurricane pilot would move his gun switch to 'fire', dive down above the beam of light and attack with the full fury of the Mk II's cannons. This was the theory. In reality, the brightly illuminated target would cast shadows which thoroughly betrayed its form. Although I only had the pleasure of mock attacks, it was obvious that the shadow-draped enemy would prove a difficult object to fire upon effectively.

This problem only became an issue if we were fortunate enough to ever get airborne. We were plagued by miserable weather and spent much of our time at the ready, milling about the dispersal hut. Again, carrots were everywhere in an effort to develop our night vision. The only result that I perceived was that I developed an absolute aversion to the orange vegetable. When we were in a position to get airborne, we would practice our interceptions and hone the co-ordination between ground radar, hunter and killer time and time again. Even so, the crews had to keep their wits about them in what was a potentially hazardous game played at very close quarters. There was one Turbinlite pilot in 536 Squadron who smoked continuously throughout these sorties and the dim red glow could be seen from the cockpit of my Hurricane quite clearly as I moved up for the attack. Perhaps he was a little nervous, or perhaps he sought to reduce the risk of collision with his additional, unofficial 'auxiliary beacon'.

The tempo of the war was ever-changing and in late 1942 the waves of marauding German bombers had thankfully disappeared. They had been replaced by lone aircraft, or 'intruders', who utilised hit and run tactics. Such an attack had accounted for a close chum of mine from my boyhood days in Glasgow. A rather gifted pilot, he was instructing a student at night in an Airspeed Oxford to the north of England. Defenceless in the twin-engined trainer, wheels down and ready to land, he was set upon by an intruder and crashed to earth. It was another great loss and I contacted his family, notably, a sister who had gone into nursing. Knowing the circumstances of his death and that fire had broken out on impact, I warned his sister that his state may well prove distressing to his parents and thought she had best view the body first, given her medical background. Thankfully, she did this and saved his parents further anguish.

Such intruder attacks were an effective weapon in terms of morale, but strategically of little consequence. The only successful Turbinlite operation in this period that I was aware of led to the demise of one such intruder. The lone Ju88 was scooting at low level over the flat lands of Norfolk when it was picked up on radar and a Turbinlite pairing was vectored to intercept. Closing to minimum range, the call of "Boil!" was made and the blinding beam was switched on, illuminating the Hun flying low and ahead. It obviously caught the German pilot by total surprise and had the result of thoroughly confusing him. Suspecting that it was a ground searchlight that had lit him up from directly behind, the cornered pilot shoved his control column forward to escape what he interpreted as a dangerously high nose attitude. What he succeeded in doing was spearing his Junkers nose down into one of England's green and pleasant lands. It was a kill, but hardly an endorsement of Turbinlite tactics.

For the most part it was practice drill after practice drill. These drills could also prove lethal as I found one evening when I was flying in company with a newly arrived Boston. Close in, I focused my attention on the tiny lights stretching back from the bomber's wing. Almost hypnotised by their glow, the strips of light would dim as we skipped through patches of cloud. I held station steadily, though this was becoming increasingly difficult as the cloud patches became thicker. With a rush, the Boston seemed to roll into a bank and then...gone! Punching into heavy cloud, I lost sight of the lights completely and attempted to pull away from the last known position of the Boston to avoid a pile up. I transferred my glazed eyes from searching for the glowing pinpricks to scanning my Hurricane's instrument panel. The transition was not smooth and the surreal tumbling of disorientation and vertigo began to dance in my head. To the din of thrashing rain my Hurricane flicked into a spin and toppled my instruments, rendering their information worse than useless. Spinning to earth in a black, wet vacuum I knew I was in dire straits. Thoughts of bailing out again crossed my mind. As quickly as I'd entered the cloud, I broke clear, though I was still spinning at a disconcerting rate. Through one rotation I glimpsed a searchlight cone reaching up from the ground, not so far below. It was all I needed to convince my brain of up from down and start recovering my tumbling fighter. Opposite rudder, steady in the dive and finally back to level flight. I'd survived another near miss, but even as I flew back to base I was convinced that the Boston was the place to be for this dance in the darkness.

I attempted to convince the CO of my suitability to fly the Boston on a regular basis. One complaint that surfaced from time to time was that the bomber pilots didn't have a thorough appreciation of close formation flying with fighters and the demands that were subsequently placed on the Hurricanes in their team. I assured the boss that I could bring this 'insight' to the table and shortly thereafter traded seats for the Boston. Prior to this, most of my multi-engine experience was on the ergonomic nightmare, the Blenheim, with only a taste of the Havoc and Beaufighter. By comparison, the Boston was a dream. Switches for the same system were grouped together and had different toggles which allowed identification by touch. It was fast, it was strong, it was built to fly.

I had borne witness to its strength a few weeks previously when a Boston had made a rather ungracious arrival back at our field. Under the control of one of our Polish pilots, the aircraft slowed at an unacceptable height above the runway and landed very heavily before entering a series of bounces. The poor chap at the wheel must have tensed up and depressed the toe brakes, a characteristic of American-built aeroplanes. Locking up all wheels fully, the aircraft started to skid and announce its arrival with a succession of bangs as the tyres blew out. Flat to the rims, sparks subsequently began to pour forth from the dragging wheels before the bomber finally came to a halt. Despite the abuse, all that was required was a change of wheels and the Boston was on its way. I believed this was how aeroplanes should be built.

By December of 1942 I was comfortable in my new role as the hunter and managed to get a reasonable amount of flying in, though it seemed that the Hun had virtually disappeared from our night skies. Scrambles for intercepts would invariably prove to be friendly aircraft and once again the frustration of Aldergrove and the monotony of OTU began to creep in. Technology was also catching up with the Turbinlite. Better radar and better aircraft, such as the Beaufighter, were taking night-fighting to a higher level. The writing was on the wall for our hunter-killer combination and as the new year dawned word came that the squadron was to be disbanded. I don't think many of us were surprised or saddened by the news. The relatively cumbersome pairing of bomber and fighter had proved ineffective and the ever-present danger stemmed from the potential for collision and not from our foe.

I missed the last rites of 536 Squadron on January 25th 1943 as I was on a short leave, though my orders arrived to report to yet another squadron in February. Variety is the spice of life and again I was destined for a new type and a new style of operation. I must admit that on first advice, I regarded my new posting as potentially a backward step. I was being sent to fly an aircraft of which I knew very little, other than it being constructed of wood. I did not realise that it was the beginning of a long relationship with one of the finest aircraft I was ever to meet. The de Havilland Mosquito.

CHAPTER TEN

Meeting the Mosquito: Down to Earth... Again

I met my new mount on February 1st 1943. As I approached the Mosquito at close quarters for the first time, I must admit, I was impressed by its beautiful lines. My reservations about its wooden construction seemed to dissipate somewhat in much the same manner that you allow a mischievous child some latitude on first meeting. There was something distinctly de Havilland about its form, yet it bore none of the 'rag and tube' traits that one associates with that earlier generation of machine with which I had first encountered the sky.

As I cast my gaze over the tall, twin-engined fighter-bomber, my cohort was my friend, Trevor Bryant Fenn. He was now 'B' Flight commander at 264 Squadron and was to be responsible for my introduction to the Mosquito. As was the way of the times, conversion training was minimal to say the least. In fact, my logbook entry for my first flight with Trevor states simply, "watching things". The Mosquito was a single pilot operation, so having given the aircraft a thorough once over on the ground, 'Fenners' strapped into the pilot's seat and I sat one place removed in the recess for the navigator. Running through the engine start procedure, one propeller started to turn slowly, blade after blade before the Merlin engine burst into harmonic life and hummed its merry tune. Without delay we fired up the second engine and started to move off towards the runway. Even at such a reserved pace as one taxies an aeroplane, I could sense the Mosquito was anxious to leap into the air. My previous British multi-engine aeroplane had been the under-powered Blenheim which had to be coaxed aloft; this was not the case with the Mosquito.

Lined up and with checks complete, Fenners opened the throttles with the sweet accompanied roar of two V12 engines. Keeping straight with finesse on the rudder, it seemed a blink before we had the speed to lift the tail and, shortly thereafter, part company with the earth altogether. Clear and free, the wheels were selected up and now I could sense the Mosquito was in its element. From that first take-off I was in awe of the aircraft's performance. Fenners wheeled it about the sky and demonstrated both ends of the 'flight envelope'. It was quite a comprehensive flight with minimal verbal accompaniment, allowing the aircraft to speak its own language. All too soon we returned to RAF Colerne, where a few circuits were demonstrated before taxiing the aircraft back in and parking on the line.

Fenners asked if I had any questions, to which I replied in the negative. This was taken as 'endorsement complete' and I was instructed to strap myself into the sole pilot's seat. I started her up and moved off under power to a nonchalant wave from my now land-locked instructor. Alone and excited, I repeated the dose of power at runway's end and roared into life. Free and clear, I was thankful for my fighter pilot heritage as the Mosquito whistled around the circuit with me working hard to keep pace with power settings, configurations and checklists. Wheels and flaps down, I swung the wooden wonder around to align with the airfield. On approach, speed and powered up, the runway grew larger in the windscreen as I started to throttle back and raise the nose for the landing. The rudder seemed to lose its effectiveness somewhat at this stage and keeping straight became a definite priority. Just as a hint of concern rose, I felt the wheels touch and the roll out began with me paying due respect, remembering that a tail wheel landing doesn't end until the aircraft is parked. I returned to a waiting Fenners who seemed pleased enough with my effort and deemed me proficient on type. My next step was to be paired up with a navigator and sent on operations.

For the second time since arriving at 264 Squadron, my crew was known to me. Warrant Officer Bernard Cannon and I had flown together previously at 536 Squadron in the days of the Turbinlite 'experiment'. He was a good man and a very competent operator, I was fortunate to be paired up with him once again. Our commanding officer was a wing commander, with whom I was not so enamoured. He had a reputation of aiming to please Operations regardless of weather and circumstance. He would continually reassure ops that, "My pilots will fly in anything." Unfortunately for Bernard and I, they took him at his word.

The night of April 23rd 1943 was bleak, to make an understatement. Low thick cloud had descended on the area and regular, torrential rain thrashed against the windows of our huts. The weather was widespread across England and squadrons had been stood down accordingly. The only crew at readiness was McGlashan and Cannon. We were sitting in the dispersal hut discussing the foul night outside and our boredom within when it was agreed that we might as well catch up on our sleep. We had just nodded off when the dispersal hut door swung open with an accompaniment of wind and water that poured forth into our digs. As the door was forced shut against mother nature, Bernard and I sat up to see what was causing the commotion. Standing there, very damp and a little disillusioned by the sight of his comatose crew, was our wing CO. He had made his way from the mess to see how we were faring and found that, in our opinions, we were faring very well. Unimpressed, he rang ops and repeated his war cry of, "My pilots will fly in anything." Then he left.

A short time later, that same phone rang. It was ops and we were being scrambled. A single suspect hostile aircraft had been observed by radar crossing the Channel and heading towards our piece of coastline.

Bernard and I faced the elements and fought our way to our regular Mosquito, number 304. Just getting to our aircraft was a battle as wind, rain and mud conspired against us in a quartering attack. Ready to go, I eased the power up carefully, pleading with the wheels to start turning over the waterlogged earth. Finally free, we made our way to the runway and took off to the deafening sound of rain on the windscreen. Just airborne and raising the gear we flew into the low overcast which must have been sitting at only a few hundred feet and turned onto our interception vector. Rolling out on the heading our aircraft began to take on an eerie blue glow. We were swathed in St. Elmo's fire as we punched through the heavy, dark gloom of this miserable English night. The windshield, propellers and leading edges of the wings seemed particularly at the mercy of the phenomenon to the degree that the windscreen was rapidly becoming opaque. I was scanning my instruments constantly when the first bumps were encountered. These rapidly developed into the most violent turbulence I have ever flown in, including the monsoonal thunderstorms I would encounter later in my career. We were being absolutely hammered by the conditions and Bernard and I heaved on our harnesses to avoid being thrown into the Perspex canopy. It was becoming exceedingly difficult to control the Mosquito and I began to wonder about the integrity of its all wooden construction when Bernard picked up a 'blip' on his radar.

A lone blip. We and one other fool were the only aircraft daft enough to be challenging the weather's fury. Bernard called a course and we closed to minimum range behind the target. What would normally be larger than life and dead ahead was now invisible through the weather and our St. Elmo's wrapped windscreen. We could not make visible contact and the turbulence again threw us about the sky like a toy. The target kept dropping off the radar and we repeatedly reacquired it, only to regain minimum range without a sighting. This game of cat and mouse took us north for thirty minutes and Bernard was getting rather sick of the whole exercise; I could not help but agree with him. Then our target, still oblivious to our presence, turned south as, realising that there was nothing to be done this night, he was setting course for home. Bernard was keen to head home as well and wanted me to open fire and be done with the whole futile exercise. Sitting at minimum range with nothing to be seen, I called control and asked if I could open fire without visual identification. They replied that I could not and shortly after instructed us to return to base. We peeled off from our foe, knowing that he was unaware how close to his demise he had really been. Now our only enemy was the weather.

We set course for Colerne on a vector provided by control, still enveloped in St. Elmo's fire. Downwards and lower we continued through the heavy cloud without any sign of breaking clear. I continued to scan my instruments vigorously, only glancing up in an attempt to see if we had broken the weather's shackles. Still nothing. I began lowering flap and gear in anticipation of landing and prayed the controller had lined us up with the runway as the altimeter only had a little way to go before we would be clipping trees. Approaching 300 feet, the St Elmo's slipped from our airframe and the first breaks in the cloud began to appear. Soon after, the first stages of

Drem's approach lighting began to appear and I was able to orientate myself with the airfield. I flew from light to light, finding the funnel lights and then, finally, the angle of approach indicator. It glared back that we were in the red sector and dangerously low; something I already knew. It stayed red until I passed the indicator at which time I pulled the throttles and set Mosquito 304 back on the ground.

Back at dispersal, I shut the aircraft down. Bernard flung the door open, climbed down the ladder, knelt and kissed the sodden ground. His actions spoke for both of us. The total flight time had been one hour twenty minutes and was one of the most terrifying experiences of my life. It had been immensely frustrating that we were even flying that night, not to mention a minimum range interception without firing. My total dependence upon instruments was challenged at every turn by the genuine chance that the turbulence could topple my clocks at any second. We had eluded death in so many ways that night for what seemed a fairly pointless exercise. Later the controllers told me that our Mosquito was the only allied aircraft flying at that time and wondered why.

Our CO definitely wasn't flying, he rarely ever did. In fact we were at a loss why he was so upset when Fenners bumped his aircraft taxiing in on the blackest of nights a short time later. Thankfully we had a change of commanding officers and welcomed Wing Commander 'Marmy' Allington as our new boss. He was a charming man who socialised with his squadron and actually flew on operations. Things were looking up.

*   *   *

As with all new postings, the shift to 264 Squadron at Colerne had been another move for Doreen as well as me. Our first daughter, Jane, had been born in January, so it was as a family that we now sought new lodgings. In true form Doreen handled the exercise with due diligence and once again, called upon our landlady from Charmy Down and my night-fighting days of 87 Squadron. Doreen recalls the time from her viewpoint:

> On February 1st 1943, Mac was posted to 264 Squadron at RAF Colerne, near Bath. Our circuit of the same stations then began, so it was off to Mrs Corbett in Marshfield again, though this time I had a small baby as well. She had no hesitation and

welcomed us back to her home; bless her! We
enjoyed our time at Colerne as 264 was a fantastic
squadron and we made many good friends. Not
many wives travelled around with the squadron, it
seems they preferred to stay put in a house
somewhere without all the hassles of a move every
three months which is the average time a squadron
stayed in any station. I didn't agree with this
thinking as so many of our pilots were 'getting the
chop' and we enjoyed being together in the same
place with whatever time we had. There were some
memorable parties at Colerne, one summer ball in
particular. My special friend Betty Bryant-Fenn wife
of Mac's flight commander Trevor Bryant-Fenn or
'Fenners' as he was always called, was sitting with
me watching some sort of cabaret, all dolled up in
our best evening dresses. From behind us a
handsome young pilot, Mike Muir, raised his
tankard to the ceiling, spilling most of his beer down
the back of our necks and shouting "I'm twenty-one
today, I'm twenty-one today". There followed a wild
chase up the staircase and corridors of this beautiful
old stately home, which was the mess, and people
were shooting off Verey pistols all over the place. I
think a lot of chaps didn't expect to live long enough
to have to answer for their wild behaviour. Poor
Mike eventually failed to return from a sortie across
the Channel a few months later.

Whilst Doreen visited her mother in Richmond, I kept busy
becoming more and more at home on the Mosquito. Much of
the time was spent honing my skills on mock drills as genuine
scrambles were fairly infrequent at that time. We would
practice interceptions on 'friendly foe' and engage in air-to-air
gunnery that only fired frames of film when the trigger was
pulled. Routinely we would be called upon to test fly aircraft
that had been in for routine maintenance or repairs of some
other description. On May 5th 1943, they wheeled Mosquito
Mk II 4080 out of the hangar and asked me to take her for a
run to see if the bugs had been ironed out. The task *seemed*
simple enough.

Bernard and I had just settled in after take-off when a loud bang got our attention. My first thought was that someone was firing on us and had scored a very worthwhile hit. I immediately rolled the 'Mossie' into a split-arse turn and dove, scanning for another aircraft. Conscious of a change in the handling of my machine, it soon became evident that I was losing power on the port engine. Still no enemy to be seen, I spotted a gaping hole in my left engine cowling from which oil was now spewing out. I shut the engine off and feathered the propeller, leaving the port airscrew stationary and edge on to the airflow. I was starting to suspect an offending engine as opposed to a Messerschmitt and warily leveled the aircraft out with Bernard and I still hunting the horizon for Huns.

This was all new territory. At no stage of my Mosquito training or operational flying had I received any instruction or experience in single-engine flying. With one Merlin dead to the world and the other pounding out 1500 horsepower the asymmetric forces were being kept at bay through the rudder via my right boot. I had lost speed and felt very vulnerable to attack should we have company in the sky at any time. My situation was compounded by the radio failing and being unable to contact any of the ground controllers or, for that matter, anyone at all. I limped my broken Mosquito back to base just in time to see a resident squadron of Australian Beaufighters returning en masse from a sortie into the Bay of Biscay. The Aussie 'Beaus' would have been getting low on fuel and had their own motivation to get back on the ground. Using the shorter of the runways, one after the other the Beaufighters recovered to base as I positioned myself to make an approach in their wake.

Being aware that my available power was halved, I decided to delay the extension of my undercarriage and flaps a little in case they only served to drag me from the sky. I was becoming filled with apprehension as I wheeled towards the field, I had never even seen an approach on one engine and now I was being asked to execute one. I looked down and I was a bit fast. "Start throwing things out", I thought as I assessed the time was right for wheels and flaps. "Still fast and I'm getting high!" The gear and flaps seemed to be taking forever and in fact they were. What I had overlooked from the training that I had never received was that I now had only a single operating engine-driven hydraulic pump. With half the pumping power the extension of my now much-needed drag was twice as slow. I was coming in way too fast and way too high by my reckoning but aborting the landing and going around on one engine was not an option at this height. The fences flew past below me as did yards of valuable runway. The Mosquito finally slammed to earth near the far end and bounced high into the air. At the top of the bounce I yelled to Bernard to hang on and selected my undercarriage up in a last ditch attempt to 'belly land' the aircraft. This time the barbed wire fence at the far perimeter flashed beneath the aircraft before we again crashed to earth. We swept across the field beyond the airfield's boundary at a frightening speed and for the first split second I thought we might get away with it. Dashing my hopes with equal speed, a concrete culvert loomed ahead and the Mosquito's nose pitched down into the ditch. I remember pulling my knees up to brace myself and then nothing else.

In my absence of consciousness, the aircraft disintegrated around me. On nosing over the Mosquito had come to an abrupt halt from a speed of about 100 knots. The nose, tail and wings broke off and continued on some distance from the crippled centre section where I was still trapped. The combination of hot engines, wood and ruptured fuel tanks had led to the ignition of two fires which were threatening to start raging brush fires. Nearby was my trusty navigator, Bernard Cannon, who was running around lifting gorse bushes and calling my name in a desperate attempt to locate his pilot. On impact, Bernard had been thrown out, minus his shoes, through the gaping hole where the nose cone had been. He had come to rest amongst the burning wings, miraculously sustaining only minor bruises and scratches.

I was not so fortunate. My sutton harness had broken and I had finished rolled into a ball within the mangled mess of a cockpit. The first chaps to arrive could find no trace of me and had assumed that I had followed Bernard's path of exit. My chin was forced down onto my chest and I was slowly but surely choking to death. Then someone caught a glimpse of my collar. It was inconspicuously protruding from beneath the armour plate and radio unit which had broken their moorings and piled on top of me. As the faint exchange of air gurgled from my lips, Wing Commander Gibb arrived on scene and I believe that it is to him that I owe my life. There was no lifting tackle available and I was being crushed to death in my current predicament. The wing commander had every available man come to my aid and lift the wreckage from me by hand, whilst others weaved in and dragged my seemingly lifeless body from the wreck which was strangling me.

My next recollection was a bright light. I thought, "This is it McGlashan!" For a moment I thought I was to meet my maker until I became aware of others scurrying about the hospital ward and busying themselves about my person. I was in excruciating pain and felt a marked reluctance to regain consciousness. The fight seemed almost too tough; perhaps it was the anaesthetic. I drifted away again and then in and out of consciousness as I attempted to focus on my whereabouts. It was the back of an ambulance, I tried to get my bearings but the wave of fatigue returned and I again slipped beneath the black veil of unconsciousness. In the meantime Doreen was just receiving the news:

> Late on the evening of May 5th, a police officer came to my mother's door saying that he had bad news for me. My husband had been in a serious air crash and was in the Truro Infirmary, Cornwall. So it had finally happened to me.
>
> Needless to say, the squadron was very supportive and sent Mike Muir's navigator 'Rocky' Mountain, to drive me and the baby down to Cornwall. When we arrived at the hospital it was time for the baby to feed, so I sat on Mac's bed and began to feed her, much to the amazement of the others in the ward. It was a great relief to find that by the time of my arrival, Mac was in fairly good condition and spirits.
>
> Nearby lay Mike Muir who was also in hospital recovering from a hernia operation. Far from the carousing state of his twenty-first birthday, Mike begged us not to make him laugh for fear of bursting his stitches.

My entire upper body ached from the effect of the sutton harness that had ultimately failed on impact. A variety of bruises reflected where the harness had penetrated my clothing and mae west to crush against my chest and torso. The worst injuries were to my legs. Both limbs were badly battered below the knees with accompanying deep lacerations that were to leave me with scars for life. I dearly loved the visits by Doreen and our daughter Jane. They were staying with Fenners and his family and this time together cemented our families' friendship for life.

I was to spend over a month in hospital recuperating before I would be permitted back to the squadron. We had a delightful sister in charge of the ward who would pass Guinness to us as we lay outside in the sun, healing our wounds. The ward was full of officers from all services and my particular friend through this time was an army major, who had all but recovered from a motorbike accident in which he had snapped his Achilles tendon. He would push my wheelchair for me and, towards the end of my stay, we even ventured out. On one occasion we sought to investigate Truro's market day which also meant that the pubs would be open all day. We set about a fantastic pub crawl, tasting the many different beers on offer. This of course led to nature's call at regular intervals, which was quite an exercise for a wheelchair-bound pilot. My army chum would wheel me in to the gents and lever me up to a suitable position to relieve myself, before reversing the exercise and returning me to the bar. Being scarred and in uniform brought out the generosity in our Cornish hosts who figured that providing us with hops would give us the courage to return to the war. The undoing to such a perfect day came about at dusk as we were beating a retreat from their hospitality. As the major pushed me up the hill towards the hospital, gravity would take over and we would roll back a little. It was two steps forward and one step back. Occasionally we would lose our stability altogether and go over backwards with my 'khaki propulsion unit' landing on top of me. We finally made it back to the ward, but unfortunately the entire acrobatic episode was witnessed by the senior medical officer as he drove by. On arrival we were greeted by the MO, the matron and our friendly ward sister. Whilst the latter was amused, her two senior compatriots certainly weren't and we were forbidden from ever venturing out again until our discharge.

That day arrived not too soon, though I was not yet fit to return to operational flying. 264 Squadron had moved and Doreen had, once again, astutely found lodgings for the McGlashan clan.

We found a house just outside the village of Mullion

Cove, called Four Winds. Fenners' wife, Betty, and I went to inspect the property and were met by the owner who had her face partially covered by a large handkerchief. The recently widowed owner apologised explaining that she had just returned from the dentist and escorted us around the property. It was perfect, though we noted a shack to the rear. The lady explained that since her husband's passing, the need had surfaced to move into the shack so that she could rent the house for income. (Later we would find a waist-high horde of gin bottles amongst the grass, which explained the true reason for the handkerchief in front of the poor lady's face.)

We had a lovely summer there. The house had glorious views over the distant ocean. Betty Fenners and I would visit the beach with our babies regularly, making our way down the steep rocky cliffs to the isolated coastline. It was a restricted area to visitors and was littered with the large concrete structures designed to impede any attempt of invasion.

The officers' mess was perched right on top of a cliff and had been a temperance hotel in peacetime; the walls must have been covered in shame! Mullion Cove was really an air force village and had such a wonderful holiday atmosphere as there were no tourists allowed. The whole area was very beautiful and we had many wonderful trips down to the Helford River, a great yachting resort in peacetime. The small market town of Helston wasn't far away and it was the original home of the Floral Dance about which the old song was written. On market day the pubs stayed open all day and, on one occasion, Fenner's navigator Laurie Hayden stood on the steps of the main hotel and gave a spirited rendering of that famous song much to the delight of most of the squadron and the locals in the street. At the end of a lane near Four Winds there lived a nice old Cornishman who often gave us veggies from his garden and one day he produced the biggest crayfish we'd ever seen. It was so big we had to cook it in a galvanised dustbin and it was subsequently enjoyed by many of us.

The summer was at its height and life was rather good, but it was time for me to return to flying. I was now healed from my accident and made my way back to 264 Squadron at RAF Predannack, Cornwall.

CHAPTER ELEVEN

The Second Front – D-Day

My return to operational flying wasn't immediate. After such a horrendous accident, the powers that be wisely eased me back into flying at the helm of the rather more sedate Airspeed Oxford. The small twin-engined transport was used to take young Air Training Corps cadets for flights around the countryside, a task I commenced in July of 1943. Affectionately known as 'cadet bashing', this leisurely duty had me feeling rather apprehensive. The task would often entail runs along the coastal areas of south-eastern England. There were wonderful views to be had such as Dover's white cliffs, but it was also a potential hive of activity for enemy crossing the channel. The old Oxford was unarmed and far from being able to outrun any intruders. It was with a keen eye and a forever-swivelling head that I took these youngsters on their flights of fancy.

On the 10th of September I returned to operational flying in the wonderful Mosquito and my logbook reads, "Getting finger out and hand back on type." I couldn't wait to become reacquainted with this majestic aeroplane and it didn't take long until I felt comfortable once again. My regular navigator, Bernard Cannon, had moved on since our foray into the culvert and had been posted to a well deserved rest, instructing at an operational training unit. In his place I was teamed with another experienced navigator, Flight Lieutenant Kenneth Roy Lusty, whom I came to nickname 'Lecherous' for no other reason than his double-edged surname. He had flown as a 'wireless air gunner' throughout the Battle of Britain with 25 Squadron on Blenheims and, like me, also spent some time in a Turbinlite unit. His arrival at 264 Squadron coincided with my return to operational flying and the timing served to pair us; with Lusty as my navigator/radar operator, or 'nav/rad'. Whilst the pairing may have been a simple combination of timing and logistics, I had definitely won out with the assignment. Lusty was not only a tremendous chap, he was a first rate operator who instilled confidence at every turn and this was critically important given the nature of our work.

Even operational flying in the latter stages of 1943 seemed routine. We had no successful interceptions for weeks at a time and German activity seemed at an all time low. Life consisted of never-ending patrols, searchlight co-ops and practice ground controlled intercepts (GCIs). Once again, the greatest enemy seemed to take the abstract form of boredom. In December we moved base again, this time to RAF Church Fenton in Yorkshire. I chose to live off base with Doreen and Jane at a pub called The Ulleskelf Arms. In the absence of German aircraft, the most exciting aspect of this posting was the ongoing local darts game.

Whilst this relocation possibly had genuine strategic merit, we would never know. Much of the shifting, squadron-hopping and repainting of aircraft had a less practical motivation. It was all in the battle against the enemy within; spies. If you were to believe the posters and propaganda, Britain was riddled with persons unknown, seeking to undermine the war effort at every opportunity. No end of procedures and sleight of hand had come about in an attempt to defeat this insidious foe, but more often than not only the friendly forces were inconvenienced.

The monotony of the patrols was broken late in December 1943 when I attended an instrument flying course with 1530 Beam Approach Training Flight. Here at RAF Wittering I was reunited with the Airspeed Oxford of my brief cadet bashing spell and a highly technical piece of equipment known as the 'Link Trainer'. A forerunner to today's flight simulators, this small box accommodated a lone pilot and sat a matter of feet off the floor. Inside, and void of any visual cues, the pilot would fly his 'aircraft' solely with reference to instruments. Outside, the instructor would assign tasks through a radio system and watch the student's performance as it plotted a, hopefully, not too shaky line across the chart on an adjoining table.

Here our training centred on a concept known as the beam approach. This entailed homing in on radio beacons in order to locate our airfields and subsequently guide us on our approach to land, again, solely with reference to instruments. It was the early generation of radio navigation and instrument approaches that today guides aircraft safely home all around the world. For me it was a reprieve from patrols and a chance to hone a new skill. At the course's end I was rated 'above average' and made my way back to Church Fenton to try my new skill in the real world.

And then, something finally began to stir. Early in March 1944 we were advised to send our families away, so Doreen and Jane made passage to my home in Scotland where they would reside with my parents. Back at 264 Squadron we were having a shuffle of personnel with Wing Commander Allington and my old friend, Trevor Bryant-Fenn, posted elsewhere and in their place came Wing Commander Smith and Squadron Leader Chase respectively. With our families sent to the country and increased troop and truck movements that seemed to choke the roads, it was apparent that the time was rapidly approaching for the long rumoured opening of a second front by means of an allied landing in Europe. We knew it was coming, but the how, where and when were still to be detailed.

In the midst of this activity, danger was never too far away and there were all manner of threats, many home-grown. Electrical gremlins continued to play havoc with our Mosquitos and on a couple of sorties Ken and I were forced to return without radar, radios or lights. On these occasions I would nurse the Mosquito in to land as Ken's torch beam scanned across my instrument panel to give me glimpses of the critical information needed to pilot the aircraft. In retrospect, this was a relatively good night as we once lost all of our primary instruments on approach! Hurtling down the runway at over 100 knots with no lights and no instruments is an educational experience to say the least.

Operational flying also began to take a turn for the better with the Germans attempting to venture forth once more over British soil. Furthermore, we were being increasingly tasked to refine our skills with airborne radar intercepts and, with Ken, I set about practicing in all earnest. Inspired with a new purpose and, to a degree, rid of the monotony of patrols we executed our procedures time and again. This was often done well to the north and clear of the Channel to avoid any possible detection by prying bombers or beams. As always, we were plagued by sub-standard radios which played havoc with our schedule. Poor radios had been a factor when I'd been shot down over Dunkirk in 1940 and very little had improved in the years that had since passed. We worked through the inconvenience and flew numerous intercepts upon one another and late in April practice operations commenced that were referred to simply as 'special exercises'.

May 13th saw the move south to Hartford Bridge in Hampshire, which seemed to be a suitable staging point for any upcoming activity. Various units of armour sat parked within the woods adjacent to the airfield, confirming that an invasion was nigh. Even so, Ken and I were amazed that civilian traffic still had access to the base. Despite an almost paranoid fear of spies throughout the war years, the powers that be still allowed uncontrolled vehicular movement at a front line base, although they did have to stop and give way when we taxied! For our part, we found ourselves living under canvas in preparation for a more nomadic existence on the Continent. Tent living was a new experience for we fighter pilots who had experienced the relative luxury of huts and, in my case, a home off base. To compound our newfound lifestyle, the weather turned bitterly cold and miserably wet. We squelched from our accommodation to the flight line and back again, with mud our constant companion. From time to time, Ken and I treated ourselves to eggs and bacon over in our tent, though one could not help but wonder about the hardship endured by ground troops on a daily basis and the battle that lay ahead on a frozen Europe.

We shared Hartford Bridge with other squadrons operating American-built Bostons and Mitchells, one of which was a free French unit. There was a constant throng of activity as we all set about refining our own given tasks. Significantly, aircraft started to return from routine maintenance bearing a bold new addition to their paint scheme. Black and white stripes in broad bands obliterated areas of camouflage on both the wings and fuselage. Often the letters constituting the aircraft code were obscured as well in the application of the new markings. Far from our usual scheme of concealment, the new stripes increased our visibility in an attempt to assist land and sea based gunners in telling friend from foe. Mosquito 493 had returned without such markings and I was advised that it would be painted in time. I was rather keen to be identified as 'friend' as I had been in His Majesty's Navy's line of fire at Dunkirk, Aldergrove and Dieppe with numerous near misses.

Our aircraft was not the only aspect of operations with a

new look. The runway at Hartford Bridge was equipped with FIDO. Fog investigation and dispersal operation consisted of pipes running down both sides of the runway which were pumped full of petrol. Holes were atop the pipes at regular intervals and, when ignited, created two lines of fire; I often wondered who was given the task of lighting the match! The device served to disperse fog and low cloud whilst also acting as an approach path for returning aircraft. Breaking out of cloud and being confronted by the towering lines of flame, you would descend into the inferno thinking this must be what hell looks like. It also proved a major incentive in keeping straight after touchdown, as a swing away from the centreline could see you sharing a common fate with the ultimate sinner.

Amongst the aircraft to fall at this time, one was of particular interest and significance; a Junkers 88. Ken and I actually intercepted the intruding Junkers on yet another miserable night with thunderstorms filling the sky and soaking our airfield. From an initial separation of twenty-five miles and a starting 'difference height' of 10,000 feet, we got a bead on the German in spite of the weather. Whilst never closing to firing range the offender was thankfully downed, I believe by one of our fellow squadrons. Curiously, the wreckage was found to have some 'additional equipment' on board and when dissected by our boffins, the little black box was identified as a miniature jamming device. Critically, it covered virtually all of the frequencies of our beacons and signalling devices that would be vital to any potential landing. This created a stir, if not panic, and our technical people scurried to the drawing board to hastily design a countermeasure for this unexpected development. The result was a receiver that could be adapted to fit our old fixed radar aerials on the Mosquito. In turn a reduced power transmitter was fitted and produced a signal which we were able to emit using our airborne radar with the net effect of being able to jam the jammers. We were now flying the later marques of the Mosquito and only six were to be fitted with the new anti-jamming units; one of which was mine. The crews of these selected aircraft were sworn to absolute secrecy and would be called to undertake training specific to the anti-jamming gear. Unfortunately, the time available for this training was minimal with the opening of the second front imminent. Compounding the issue, Lusty and I were without our Mosquito 493 for a short period whilst the anti-jamming gear was fitted, but on its return we busily set about our new special exercise in the limited time remaining.

The weather continued to plague our preparation, yet there was an air of genuine purpose and intent surrounding Hartford Bridge. As the invasion approached, all patrols and mock intercepts gave way to our special exercises. The day was nearing and we were ready, yet 493 sat there, an orphan child still deprived of her black and white invasion stripes. It was four years since Dunkirk and I eagerly awaited our return to Europe.

* * *

If I had been unaware of the historical significance of the events of 1940 as the British forces evacuated Dunkirk, I could not begin to grasp how our return to Europe was going to be played out time and again in the years to follow. Lusty and I had been flying busily of a night refining our intercepts, or bullseye ops, and making use of our new box of tricks. Following a hop on June 2nd, we didn't fly for the next couple of days and debated amongst ourselves what was happening. I resorted to my old friend sleep for much of the time, having learnt from experience that rest was critical, particularly if D-Day was upon us.

On June 5th, the armour concealed about the airfield perimeter seemed to be thinning out. There was movement afoot and Ken and I knew it wouldn't be long before our squadron's handful of Mosquitos, equipped with their anti-jamming gear, would be called to the ready. Our wait did not last much longer as we were versed on our role that evening at briefing; along with the other specially equipped crews we would be bound for France. We knew that our task was somewhat specialised by the presence of high-ranking officers flitting about the operations hut.

There was still great reserve that the equipment found on the Ju88 might disturb our plans for D-Day. If they were to jam our frequencies, all sorts of havoc could be played with the invasion force and its co-ordination. Just as in my cat's eye nights when our radar stations were able to bend the beams of approaching bombers, the German jammers could turn the tables on our plans. Critical paratroop deployments could end up dropped miles from their selected targets; already a big enough problem with just the weather as a factor. Our task was to cross the Channel and fly in ever increasing circles, hunting for any sign of the German 'radio warriors'. Should we detect a signal, we were to home in on it and attack the sender, just as we had been rehearsing in our special exercises, but with a major difference. We were briefed that we were to attack until all of our ammunition was expended and then ram the enemy if need be. Failing this, we were to chase the target until the point of fuel exhaustion, again in an attempt to ram them. Following such mid-air conflict we were to bale out and join the Resistance. I raised the issue that our Mosquito had not yet had its camouflage modified in line with the other aircraft, to which I received a succinct response that it would be night and would make no difference. I must agree, it seemed to be somewhat of a side issue.

Whilst we were assigned to hunt over France behind the beachhead, from St. Pierre, near Caen, to St. Martin, meanwhile, the war of deception would be taking place elsewhere. Bombers would be dropping foil to send erroneous images of a phantom bomber force back to German radar. This was intended to mask Normandy as the landing point and suggest a site further north, like Calais. Throughout the prelude to the invasion, attacks on German assets had taken place all along the French coast to prevent any suggestion of the point of landing. The fact that we were to be patrolling in skies that were still owned by the Luftwaffe was not lost on us and we had a degree of trepidation about wandering around their backyard. If we had reservations, we could only wonder what was going through the minds of the landing force as they set course for France. If it was going to be tough for us, I could only pity the chaps who were chopping their way across the Channel in boats and barges.

The first two crews were airborne that evening at around 11pm. A little after midnight, we folded up the wheels on 493 and scooted outbound, low towards the coast. Crossing the Channel we peered into the darkness but could not make out the invasion force, pounding its way through the waves. At the time the moment was lost on me as I was occupied with the task at hand, but I had witnessed our withdrawal from France and was now playing a part in our return. The Dunkirk evacuation had been a flotilla of odds and sods desperately shuttling troops to the safety of Britain by any means possible. Tonight Operation Overlord, as it would come to be known, was a vast coordinated effort that was long in the making. Our anticipation had given way to a sense of purpose and now the day had arrived. Unlike many of my comrades from those first days of flying training, I had survived to see this day eventuate.

Under a veil of radio silence that added to the solemnity of the event, we whistled through the buffeting winds as the French coast approached and I spared a thought for my abandoned Hurricane now being lapped by the tide. Easing up the power, I raised the nose and the Mosquito hurtled skyward and made for a point ten miles inland between St. Pierre and St. Martin. Perched at 30,000 feet, Ken was head down, working plots and scanning his gear for any trace of activity. At this height we had excellent radar coverage but, with the exception of our fellow 264 Squadron Mosquitos, we seemed to be the only aircraft in the skies. For three hours we sought out any evidence of German signals or jamming devices and registered nothing. Our excitement was giving away to frustration as we worked our way further and further northward until we were virtually over Paris. I was pondering the meaning of this non-event. Did we genuinely have an element of surprise, or was the enemy lying low and waiting for us in his den? We suspected that maybe our bombers had done their job in the 'softening up' that preceded D-Day. Whatever the cause, we encountered nothing at all until we turned for home and started to pick up the foil being snidely dropped by our own bombers. To our radar the 'chaff' painted a very impressive strike force that never was!

As we let back down to Hartford Bridge the weather was not ideal. Down and down we continued and still there was no sign of gaining visual reference to the ground. We broke out from the low cloud base at a few hundred feet only to be confronted by a sea of gliders in our path. I advanced the throttles and poured on the coals sending the Mosquito back into the gloom. Cleaning up the gear and flap we received belated advice from the controller to 'hold' and he would advise when it was clear to land. I checked our fuel status and we had adequate reserves to comply with the controller's instruction for the moment, but could not escape the fact that our mission had almost come to a grievous end returning to our home base. After an absence of drama over the Continent we had been adequately compensated at Hartford Bridge. Without too much further delay, we were advised that our approach path was now clear and the gliders had started their long tow to Europe. This time on breaking clear we continued on and reunited the Mosquito with mother earth once again. It was now after 4am and I was a little weary as we taxiied in. For all of the anticipation, our sortie had been seemingly a 'milk run'. This in itself may have provided worthwhile information as we de-briefed the mission and its associated weather to the keen ears of the intelligence staff and subsequently our fellow officers. By the time we arrived back at our tent, it was the small hours of June 6th and I knew the troops would be approaching the beaches. We had little idea of what would transpire, though we were aware that it would not be easy. Fatigued, and a little reflective, I stretched out and drifted off into a very deep slumber.

It was still overcast, but there was no stopping the light creeping through every crack and the wind flapping every panel of our tent. Almost as soon as my eyes opened we were ordered over to briefing for details of the day's operations. The roar of engines confirmed that the invasion was in full swing and all forms of air power were being thrown across the Channel. That evening it was back to briefing and our task for D-Day was a 'special patrol of the second front – France' and that's just how I entered it into my logbook. Tonight our beachhead patrol was to centre on Cherbourg and again we were seeking out the enemy's exponents of electronic warfare.

This time in 477 we took to the air and again it was around midnight. Frustratingly the action at Normandy was once again concealed by weather and the veil of darkness. For over an hour we hunted uneventfully, though we did intercept a couple of our own Lancasters. Not long after our friendly encounter, Ken advised me that the radar gear had failed. We now had what we referred to as a 'bent weapon' and there was not much decision making required at this point as our Mosquito had been rendered useless. I wheeled the Mossie over and made a direct line for Hartford Bridge as Ken called the heading. We scooted back across the Channel leaving history to take its course without us.

It would be June 10th before we would be back over France. By this time the allied advance had moved well north towards Caen. Lusty and I continued to search the skies and continued to find nothing. With the invasion at Normandy accomplished, the RAF sought to keep pace with the ground forces. This would mean the basing of squadrons on the Continent for the first time since the Battle of France in 1940 and 264 was in line for the move. My fate lay elsewhere as I, along with two other crews, was adjudged 'tour expired'; or 'tourex'. I had been flying operationally since 1939, though the chance of this continuing seemed bleak as my name was submitted to the air ministry for posting.

When the verdict was handed down I was offered an instructional position at an operational training unit. Memories of monotony and frustration came flooding back as I recalled my time at 60 OTU and East Fortune. I asked if there was anything else available and there was indeed.

CHAPTER TWELVE

BOAC

I had flown from Dunkirk to D-Day and now, in mid-June of 1944, it was decided that my operational flying days were to draw to a close. From the outset I had been a fighter pilot, be it in day, night or foul weather operations. Other types of flying bordered on being alien to me, though they were still a preferable option to being deskbound. Whilst I was to take a step back from the rigours of combat, the RAF weren't overly forthcoming with any rest and recreation. As such, a fortnight after my last patrol over the second front I found myself in the stark belly of a Consolidated Liberator destined for Egypt.

As we made our way south, the four-engined bomber whistle-stopped in Gibraltar on the southern tip of Spain before taking off once again and heading westward across the Mediterranean. North Africa had been the scene of the desert war and seemed almost removed from the conflict I'd participated in over Europe. It had been the realm of Rommel, the 'Desert Rat', and his Afrika Corps which had finally been defeated only a year before. To traverse these skies unescorted in those times would not have been an option, yet now the Luftwaffe had recalled its remaining units to Europe and we lumbered along in the relative comfort of air supremacy. We reached Almaza airfield, to Cairo's east, in the still of night and were offloaded like so much human freight before being directed to our temporary lodgings in the appropriately named Heliopolis Palace Hotel. I had arrived in the Middle East; my home for the next eighteen months.

I was one of a group of RAF pilots who were now on secondment to No. 2 Division of our national airline, the British Overseas Airways Corporation (BOAC). Shortly after our arrival in Egypt we commenced our ground training in all manner of subjects including celestial navigation. Drummed into us by imposing figures with four gold bars, these were obviously new and uncharted waters to a pilot whose longest hops had previously only taken him as far as France where map reading, beam flying and common sense had sufficed. However, these were different times and airline operations were scaling up in preparation of a world without war. Civil aviation was commissioned to link the continents and our primary task was to be the opening of the air routes through the Middle East. The aircraft we were to fly were a far cry from the high performance fighters I had been used to. Armstrong Whitworth Ensigns, Douglas Dakotas, Shorts Flying Boats and the like were being used to defeat another enemy; the tyranny of distance. These were large, long-range, multi-engined machines whose cockpit was shared by two pilots; a totally foreign concept for me. Furthermore, on completion of my training I was to become a co-pilot, or first officer. I had always commanded my aircraft since my earliest days with 245 Squadron and now I was to be the apprentice rather than the master. This in itself was to prove an exercise in diplomacy as I was to learn as time progressed. It was now September and, for the moment, it was one step at a time. With my theory lessons behind me I returned to flying and set about my conversion onto the Lockheed 18, or as we knew it, the 'Lodestar'.

Under the watchful eye of Captain Lipkin I became familiar with the Lodestar through a series of local flights out of Almaza. It was more a case of 'managing the engines' as the early Lodestars were powered by the temperamental Wright Cyclone powerplants, though these were later replaced with far more satisfactory Pratt and Whitney engines. The Lodestar was a versatile aircraft in ways Lockheed had never considered. When we undertook to deliver pilgrims to Mecca, a solution had to be found for the specific ablutionary needs of the passengers who were unable to defecate facing Mecca, or in the company of others. To this end, the rear quarter of the aircraft was cordoned off with a curtain and drip trays full of sand were placed on the floor. Whilst these measures met the passengers' needs and minimised the cleaners' task, the odour in the cabin was not the best.

Such were the pleasantries of early air travel. The Lodestar also had an interesting seating arrangement which consisted of two benches with their backs to the aircraft walls. As such, the passengers would face each other which made for an entertaining flight in rough weather. The catering was in the form of packed lunches stowed at the cabin's rear and no sooner would we become airborne than the cry for meals would ring out and I would slip back to fill another of the first officer's crucial roles. Well into a flight from Addis Ababa to Asmara at 15,000 feet we encountered the usual severe turbulence. The full stomachs in the cabin did not sit well with the heaving airframe and the passengers sat quietly, face to face, watching each other become greener and greener. At the point of critical mass, the first passenger yielded and retched a torrent from deep within and so set off a chain reaction. As I viewed the scene over my shoulder it resembled twin fountains cascading from each side of the narrow cabin. Once again, spurred on by the incessant heat, the odour was overpowering.

Back in Cairo, with three other pilots, I had moved from the luxurious Palace Hotel to more modest, yet spacious, lodgings near the local racecourse. The flat was being let by a Belgian gentleman who was involved with the Suez Canal and the accommodation proved a windfall for us RAF pilots, making the time away from home a little easier to bear. We all got on splendidly and would bring back such treasures as Gorgonzola cheese, Cypriot brandy and Molotti beer for communal use. To keep the cheese free of ants, we would suspend it from our central ceiling light fitting. The Molotti beer possessed a rather fierce sting in its tail. Instead of using hops in its manufacture, the local brewers utilised a weed-like plant as a substitute. Unlike the excellent Egyptian Stella, anything over three pints rendered the drinker at the mercy of 'Molotti's Pipe' which produced a frequent urge to urinate that would go on for hours.

Our 'house man' was Amin and a fine chap he was, though a tough taskmaster when he was training his twelve-year-old nephew as an assistant. The lad's name was unpronounceable, though we modified it to 'Stumblebum'. On completion of Stumblebum's duties, primarily cleaning and dusting, Amin would sweep in majestically in his long white flowing 'Gelbia' to inspect his work. He would lift the hem and wipe the underside of a table and woe betides if Amin's gown emerged soiled. He would kick and pursue the luckless apprentice upstairs to the family dwelling on the roof from where a tirade of Arabic abuse would echo. Next day they would be cheerful and once again on the best of terms. Amin purchased our food and provided any other goods we needed and on reviewing our accounts, it was obvious that Amin was as honest as the day is long. He cooked our meals, laundered our clothes, woke us with a cheerful smile and retrieved us when we staggered home at some ungodly hour. He was valet, cook, butler, mine of information and friend.

The region was not the safest in this period as the Egyptians were seeking their independence from the British. Travel on foot or alone by taxi was risky and any form of carelessness was an open invitation to robbery, injury or worse. At this time we all carried a fly whisk which concealed a knife or blackjack as a last line of defence. I once witnessed an angry mob being dealt with outside one of our military establishments where they had gathered. Without warning, British commandos burst through the huge gates and set about dispersing the crowd. The rioting Egyptians were no match for the trained soldiery and they were soon on their way without a single shot being fired. This group was more fortunate than those who sought to besiege a Ghurka base at a later date. They had sought to blockade the compound by obstructing the entry road with their bodies, but failed to count upon a determined Ghurka driver who gained access straight over the top of the protesting assembly.

From the Lodestar one would graduate to the somewhat larger Ensign. With a gross weight in excess of twenty-two tons, forty passengers and four radial engines it was a step up in size from all of my previous types. Even so, we covered our vast network at speeds less than three miles per minute which is a far cry from today's 747s that shrink the globe at three times this speed with hundreds on board. For the pilots, the Ensign was a monster. It was a heavy, under-controlled pig to fly in rough monsoon conditions and the only aircraft that I ever flew that literally could give one blisters! In such weather it summoned the combined strength of both pilots and this led to an incident as we approached Calcutta's airport, Dum Dum. I had left the cockpit to ensure that the passengers were strapped in for landing, only to find that one Indian gentleman was missing. I eventually ascertained that he was in one of our lavatories and set about banging on the door to gain his attention without success. The earth grew big in the window and the aircraft continued to be thrown about at all angles in the turbulence. I returned to the cockpit to assist the captain on the controls as he wrestled the beast to the ground knowing full well we had a passenger being tossed about in the rear cubicle. As soon as we cleared the runway, I unstrapped and returned to the lavatory where the occupant finally opened the door. The entire contents of the Elsan toilet had been ejected in the turbulence and spread liberally over the walls, ceiling, floor and one very wretched passenger. Without a word I closed the door and returned to the cockpit where I informed the captain of the hideous state of affairs. The cleaners were organised to board promptly and attend to the aircraft and our hapless gent.

Our routes took us in all directions from Cairo. Bounded by Tehran, Calcutta, Istanbul, Ankara and Bulawayo, we serviced all points within. It was a far cry from Bearsden, Dumbartonshire! A typical trip would depart Almaza for Baghdad, Bahrain, Sharjah, Karachi, Delhi and Calcutta with numerous other stops along the way. Over ten days we would fly around twenty-five sectors in fifty hours behind the wheel with possibly a couple of days off, or 'slip', in foreign ports. We also travelled south into Africa and serviced ports such as Nairobi in Kenya and Khartoum in Sudan. However, for all the miles that slid beneath there was unfortunately very little time to explore these exotic ports. Arriving late and departing early the next morning, the best chance of sightseeing would lie in unforeseen aircraft breakdowns. A failing magneto or tired cylinder was often a ticket to explore the history of Damascus or Luxor.

We weren't totally without interaction with the locals throughout the region. The Gully Gully men were members of an incredible tribe that lived some distance away in the sandy ports. These gentlemen would conjure your belt, lift your wallet and produce day old chicks from your ears. As acrobats they would lie down and juggle small children with their upturned feet. In the urban regions we would frequent Arab cafes where smokers sat in groups inhaling through their 'hubbly bubbly' water pipes, entertained by singers and belly dancers. After a few ales one evening I inadvertently offended one of the dancers when I dropped my cigarette ash into her outstretched tambourine. The next thing I knew I had the instrument's wooden ring around my neck and things had become a little hostile. I hastily remedied the situation with a generous tip followed by my speedy departure.

For the most part, the flying was quite hard work. Conditions in those times were very primitive by today's standards. We and our passengers were totally without all the aids and comforts now regarded as a necessary part of commercial flying. You could say we were, quite literally, flying by the seat of our pants. Our most sophisticated navigational aid was a loop aerial, designed to provide the crew with directional information on a cockpit-mounted instrument, however the external aerial usually iced up. This rendered the device absolutely useless during dreadful weather, at the very time we needed it most. Even my old friend, 'dead reckoning' proved difficult in an atmosphere thick with rising sand. Our sole foray into the world of high technology was via the most basic of autopilots which was fitted to most aircraft. Again, adverse weather conditions effectively disabled this device too. In turbulence, the system would easily topple and the aircraft would obediently follow and therefore it was only used sparingly.

Not even breathing could be taken for granted, so we seldom flew over 15,000 feet as the aircraft was unpressurised and the supply of oxygen reduced. Even at this level the atmosphere is rarified and marginally capable of supporting life and rational thought. We carried small portable cylinders of the life giving gas for the passengers in case of an emergency. One of my duties as the first officer was to keep an eye out for any passenger judged to be in need of revival. If I recognised any hypoxic signs such as blue lips or unconsciousness, I would dart back to the cabin and administer a few life giving breaths of oxygen from the hand-held cylinder. However, if the weather was bad or we were pushing through heavy turbulence, the passengers' comfort came second to more pressing issues such as keeping the aircraft upright.

Our flying height limitations also ensured that there was little chance of climbing over bad weather as airliners do today. Consequently we had the choice of ploughing straight through the murk or dodging along beneath it. Both were very hazardous options in the tropical storm conditions that plagued our routes. We learned to take lightning strikes, icing and hail damage in our stride. The airfields were in their infancy and without any facilities to assist us in the approach and landing phase of our journey, so arrivals were very hazardous undertakings in bad weather. Addis Ababa was a most difficult airfield to fly into as mother nature had chosen topography over weather to provide the challenge. Sitting 6,000 feet above sea level, the runway was perched on the edge of a cliff with a steep mountain at the other end. The preference of taking off and landing into wind was abandoned as the towering peak dictated direction. Aborting a landing was not an option as one would come to grief upon the mountainside and rejecting a take-off would have one tumble off the cliff's edge. The underlying necessity was to get it right the first time.

Whilst the flying could be dangerous, the associated job could be plain difficult. As a first officer I needed broad shoulders as my duties were many and varied. During loading I had to establish the centre of gravity, it was also my responsibility to check that we had enough fuel as we had learned to mistrust guages and handlers. The fuel load was simply checked by dipping the tanks prior to take-off with a graduated wooden stick. In some of the more remote places I had to help to refuel by operating a wobble pump out of a tin as small as four gallons or sometimes a forty gallon drum of petrol. I had to produce flight plans, do pre-flight inspections (very often at over fifty degrees Celsius in the shade!) and then sit dripping in the cockpit waiting to receive, report to and comfort the captain when he arrived complaining about the warmth of the lemonade in the refreshment hut. He would then draw on his white kid gloves for take-off, sitting in his special 'Koolseat' and admonish me for my dirty disheveled and more than damp appearance. Finally he would enquire if 'Mister' was ready for take-off and set about getting underway. By this time the temperature in the cabin, with all the hatches shut, would be rising rapidly to beyond boiling point. Roaring down the runway with the hot thin air starving the engines and wings of their potential, I hoped and prayed that we would get airborne without incident. I would watch the twin streams of sweat pouring off the captain's elbows as he laboured to coax the aircraft into the air, all the while supported by me holding the throttles open, raising the undercarriage or flaps and giving courses to fly. Finally free of the surly bonds and flying away, I then had to go back and distribute lunch boxes to the passengers, check the toilet and finally return to the cockpit where I would complete the technical and navigation logs which required entries every twenty minutes.

We could appear a rather rag-tag bunch as we had a choice of three uniforms; RAF, BOAC or casual attire. It was not only indicative of our varied backgrounds, but also enabled a change of identity should we wish to return to a club we had previously been asked to leave. Such was the nature of the personnel on the frontier of BOAC operations in the Middle East. I must admit, at times it was hard to play the role of second in command to some of the chaps who had far less real experience and often an arrogant attitude to match. One such gentleman lacked many of the basic skills in the area of hands-on flying and placed an unrealistic level of reliance upon our rudimentary autopilot. On one occasion we were being hammered on all fronts by weather and turbulence as rain thrashed loudly against the windscreen. Between the jolts and bolts, the aircraft would pitch, heave and roll as the automatic pilot struggled to keep up. At the limits of its ability and threatening to roll us on our back, I suggested that it may be prudent to hand fly the aircraft. Not only were the gyros set to topple but we were being pounded down to altitudes that corresponded perilously with upper realms of the surrounding hills. My suggestion was promptly ignored. Shortly thereafter we were again pummelled and sent rolling further down towards the terrain with the associated sounds of terror filtering through from the passenger cabin. I'd had enough at this point and decided to intervene. Relegating the automatics to spectator, I set about getting the aircraft under control, powering it up and pointing skyward. On reaching a safe level I nosed the Ensign over and proceeded to hand fly the aeroplane to our destination without a single objection or complaint from my rather pale captain. On reaching the safety of the parking bay, he then proceeded to unleash a tirade on the subject of my insubordination. This was in turn supported by a written report on our return, though the senior pilot did not seem interested and took no action against me. The incident seemed to have been limited to the captain's dissatisfaction and nothing more formal was registered. Not long after, the very same captain was lost with all on board when his aircraft flew into terrain. Quietly I wondered whether the autopilot was engaged at the time.

Not all of the notable experiences in BOAC related directly to the flying. We were pioneering routes in places new to air travel and finding their feet in the international community in more ways than one. Accordingly, in addition to standard airline equipment we carried 'goolie chits', Maria Theresa dollars and a sten gun! These were effectively our insurance policies should we come down in the wilder parts of Ethiopia, the Arabian Peninsula or the Gulf of Oman. In the unhappy event of a crash, we would first attempt to present our goolie chits which listed in a variety of languages, a reward for our safe return 'intact'. This was all dependent upon the other party not only being able to read, but understanding the languages listed. Should this prove unsuccessful, our next course of action was to offer fifty, or so, Maria Theresa dollars in an attempt to buy our safety (an itemised expense list was to be kept by the first officer of course). Again this was based upon the currency being of use to those who had discovered our wrecked aircraft. Finally, if all else failed; we were to use the sten! It was not specified whether the gun was to be used against hostile tribesmen or upon ourselves to get out of a tricky and potentially painful situation.

The war was drawing to a close across the globe and already entrepreneurs were surfacing throughout the Middle East. Whilst some were generous natives of the region who would bestow lavish cigarette cases upon the crew, others were American nationals seeking to exert their influence. From within our own ranks we had an individual who took to smuggling gold. He would parcel up his precious cargo and conceal it within the airframe. This was achieved by means of hanging small bags from any discreet fixture, including control cables! The ramifications of the latter were obvious but fortunately there was never a reported control problem, though the offender did finally pay his dues. One evening he had collected his booty and was making his way across the tarmac when he was called upon to halt by a local guard. Bearing in mind that those responsible for airport security held uniformed pilots in awe, a few well chosen words would have ended the incident. Instead the smuggler panicked, dropped his bag of gold and ran. Strangely there was never a report of the incident from officialdom's end, nor did the guard raise the matter in any public forum.

The war in Europe had ended in May and hostilities had ceased in the Pacific the following August. The war seemed a world away as we established new routes for BOAC. My dear Doreen and baby Jane seemed even more distant. I was hankering for the RAF again, but could not obtain a posting even though the air force was recruiting experienced aircrew. I was effectively trapped in Egypt. My active service had taken me over the length of my short service commission, so I applied for demobilisation and a return to the UK. It was duly approved and in October of 1945 I flew my last shuttle for the airline out of Almaza through the Turkish ports of Ankara and Istanbul and then made ready for my return home. It was appropriate that a party should mark the occasion. The issue of too much spirits and not enough quality was resolved by a fruit concoction mixed in an Ali Baba jar that resided in our apartment. After a couple of drinks we were walking on air, though I don't remember much about the evening other than a lass being rescued from a second storey ledge where she had lain down to sleep. The next morning Amin came in and asked if he could empty the jar of the mix. I think he believed it to be a lemonade and fruit mix as we didn't see him for two days and when he showed up to bid us farewell he was not too bright. My comrades had followed my lead and were homeward bound as well, so we gave Amin our spare food and cash which only increased his tearfulness at our departure.

I had not seen my family for well over a year and Britain was now at peace. I bid goodbye to the outdoor cinemas, ice cream parlours and museums. Adieu to the beggars, coffee shops and the world of airline flying. I contemplated the future as the engines droned and carried me northward. Fundamentally, I had been at war my entire adult working life and now this was no longer the case. My demobilisation meant I was now without an air force to call my own. I still had a card to play, but would it be an ace? Time would tell, for now only one thing mattered. Home.

CHAPTER THIRTEEN

Peaceful Times

My arrival home was in company with a huge bunch of bananas, still intact despite my long journey. Such a delicacy was not a sight in Britain during the war, so it was with fruit in hand that I stepped out to meet Doreen and Jane, however, being short of sterling I did tip the taxi driver two bananas. Shortly after my return I made my way to London where I promptly applied to rejoin the Royal Air Force. Whilst they welcomed me back and allowed me to retain my rank of flight lieutenant, BOAC were rather disgruntled at what they perceived as a back door exit from the secondment. I had to accept a dressing down at the hands of the airline, but that was a small price to pay as I was both at home with my family and once again a serving officer with the RAF.

Settling back into the best of the British climate, the arrival of 1946 saw me again staying one step ahead of a desk job and in a flying role. With the cessation of hostilities, there was a sea of equipment that now filled yards and airfields that had limited use in times of peace. The RAF recognised this and set about alleviating the gridlock by moving as much machinery as possible offshore and one of the groups tasked with this was No. 1 Ferry Unit at Pershore. Much of the work involved 'reversing' the lend lease arrangements of the war so the unit was consequently at America's bidding. On the 28th of January I had the pleasure of reacquainting myself with the trusty Mosquito by means of a forty-minute roar around the countryside. It was tremendous. After playing co-pilot on aircraft that operated on the lower threshold of performance, I was back in command with the power and freedom that only a fighter could offer. I was really home.

That same day I took an Airspeed Oxford for a buzz as it

was to serve as my mount to regain currency on night operations and a few days later I was lapping the field by moonlight. Things were looking decidedly like my first ferry flight would involve the old 'cadet basher' and I wondered to which exotic corner of the globe I would be making the delivery. Much to my surprise, and pleasure, I was ordered to make my way to France where I would pick up a Mosquito and deliver it to Africa. The aircraft had previously suffered some problems, but was now ready to go. This was a fantastic relief on two counts. Firstly, I loved the Mosquito and secondly, I knew my way around the dark continent from my recent stint with BOAC.

On my arrival at Istres, I discovered that the aircraft I was assigned had lost its roof escape panel at some juncture and in its place was affixed a light wooden and Perspex structure. As I lifted off at Istres there was a loud bang followed by the roar of aerodynamic noise. It was obvious that the stop gap panel just above my head had let go and through the gaping hole disappeared all of our charts, which were very nearly followed by my helmet. The cockpit filled with dust and for a time visibility was a distant memory as I struggled to fly on instruments in the chaos. The status quo eventually returned, with the exception of the continuing din, and I wheeled the Mosquito back to return to land. I advised the ground crew of the drama and strongly suggested that the appropriate hatch be fitted before another departure was attempted. As luck would have it, further unserviceabilities were found once the aircraft returned to the hangar and I was to take no further part in its delivery.

Back in England I was again assigned a delivery to Africa. A late model Mk XXVI Mosquito was wheeled out and this time I was told to make myself at home in 'KA294'. On the planned day of departure, the weather was far from ideal. Our first stage was from St Mawgan to Istres and the weather over the Channel was low and bleak. We were finally briefed on a window for departure and had no sooner got airborne than we were thrashed by the weather. We arrived over the continent and things were seemingly even worse with the weather on the ground. My navigator, Flight Lieutenant Ryan, and I decided to declare the exercise a misadventure and made our way back to Worcestershire and I was beginning to wonder if I was ever going to see Africa again. After this false start, we made another attempt at finding Istres the following day with much greater success.

Food supplies on the continent were still a very limited commodity, so for two days we dined solely on a menu of spinach and poached eggs. Departing Istres, we set course for Luqa on the island of Malta and seemed to have bid the foul weather adieu as we skipped southward. The next day we were aloft again and bound for my immediate past place of residence, Cairo. This time I wasn't hauling on the controls of an Ensign or stowed in the belly of a Liberator and the journey was far more pleasant. The Mosquito shrank mile after mile at its more than respectable pace and the view from the glass bubble seemed to go on for ever. Approaching Cairo, the landmarks became increasingly familiar and my nav obliged by paying more and more attention to my finger pointing and less to his meticulous plotting. We spent five uneventful days in Cairo as tourists before departing upon our final stages to Kenya.

The first hop took us to Khartoum and whilst the Mosquito's pace in the cruise was far more impressive than a BOAC airliner, it was becoming evident that the twin-engined fighter was not suited to the tropics in its current form. As the ambient temperature increased, the needles on the instrument panel crept into the red and I paid careful attention to nursing the engines as we flew south. Once on the ground at Khartoum, I gave the matter serious thought and decided that the next day we would depart pre-dawn to take advantage of the cooler conditions. Even so, the departure was eventful despite our best intentions and preparation. At runway's end I advanced the throttles slowly to full power and the temperature gauges climbed with vigour equal to the spinning propellers. Folding the wheels up and bound for the heavens, the temperatures continued to climb and climb beyond their safe limits. Outside the picture was not any better as the engines began to stream trails of glycol smoke as the coolant struggled and failed to control the engines' fever. I continued to climb the Mosquito gingerly until passing 12,000 feet where the temperatures began to decrease to acceptable limits and performance began to return. I wondered how on earth the Mosquito would be successfully operated out of Africa; though I was aware that tropical versions of the type had served with the Royal Australian Air Force. Perhaps the modifications were to be made when the Mosquito arrived at its new home, I thought.

After a total of eighteen hours of flight time, our arrival at Eastleigh, Kenya was met with a warm greeting that bordered upon ceremony. Following such a welcome, I imagined that the Mosquito was to form part of a fledgling post-war air force as the new owners meticulously checked and cross-checked the equipment on board. After a thorough assessment of the inventory, a local officer climbed aboard KA294 and summoned the aircraft back to life. I had some degree of trepidation as the chap had paid cursory attention to the current amount of fuel on board and knew nothing of our recent adventures at the hands of the oppressive heat. I sincerely hoped he wasn't intending to travel too far and indeed he wasn't. No sooner were the two Merlins firing than the park brake was released and he taxied away across the apron and beyond the runway to the remotest corner of the airfield where he was met by a gathering team of troops. The aircraft was then promptly set alight and burnt to the ground. I was aghast.

Shortly thereafter I was informed that this was all part of reversing the lend lease arrangement and accounting for weaponry that was surplus to requirements. It was cold comfort as I watched the wooden wonder go up like a tinder box in the knowledge that this was to be the fate of so many proud aeroplanes.

The journey back to England was courtesy of my former boss, BOAC, and shortly after my return home, I found myself again bound for France. This time I was called upon to undertake a different type of ferry flight involving a number of Tiger Moths. I hadn't flown the DH82 since my initial training in 1939, so I had to endure a ten-minute check flight to verify my level of competence. The small, trusty biplane had proved to be the backbone of pilot training throughout the Commonwealth but was not designed for flights of any great distance. As such, to fly our formation to a maintenance unit in Romorantin would call for six refuelling stops and a crossing of the English Channel. The process of refuelling was in itself an interesting experience as the airfields had, until recently, all been in the hands of the Luftwaffe. To walk unchallenged around these deserted aerodromes from which the Germans had been vanquished held a strange significance for me. The remnants of Germany's former military might were littered about with the eerie abandonment of a ghost town. The tools of trade that had once threatened British shores now sat dormant, perishing at the hands of mother nature and a simple breeze replaced the bustle of personnel.

My moments of melancholy were short lived as our time was consumed by the laborious task of fuelling by hand pump from drums. Operating at these airfields often posed other unexpected challenges from simple quarters, such as taxiing. Our Tigers were equipped with tail skids as opposed to the wheels found on later types. These skids would inherently be caught up in the steel matting found on airfields that allowed them to operate in all weathers. Our solution was to taxi everywhere with enough power to keep our tails raised and clear of entrapment. This was a challenging task which saw our formation darting around like a pack of demented birds threatening to take flight. Our technique was proven to be fallible at Le Buc airfield when our leader had his skid caught up and subsequently sheared from his Tiger Moth. The twelve of us absolutely rejected the idea of continuing without the boss and decided to extend our stay until the aircraft was repaired. This news was met with enthusiasm by one particular French officer who took us under his wing and was determined to show us a good time. That evening we participated in a devastating round of entertainment of the best and worst France had to offer; including a very posh brothel. Within the walls of this house of ill repute was a stage where, much to our embarrassment, erotic shows were performed that ultimately prompted our departure. The exception within our troop was our leader's navigator who fell onto the stage and offered his services free of charge. His kind offer was rejected and he was forced to call it an early night with the rest of us, much to his disappointment.

The journey was completed a couple of days later and then it was back home as a passenger once again. The next eight weeks saw the uneventful delivery of Oxfords and Mosquitos to their new homes or scenes of demise and with the passing of May 1946, my assignment to the ferry unit drew to a close. It was one of the shortest postings of my RAF career, but had served the crucial purpose of reinstating me to flying duties back in the UK. My journeys had taken me through lands recently held by our foe and rammed home the reality that the war was over. This was something that was rather hard to fathom whilst flying at my BOAC outpost. The burning of once valiant aeroplanes left me in no doubt that times were changing and that my future role in the RAF would be different from my duties as an operational fighter pilot in wartime. Only time was going to tell what that role would be.

*   *   *

From French fields and ferry flying I made my way to Yorkshire and the home of 54 OTU in June of 1946. I had previously taken all and sundry measures to keep from returning to a training unit, but I could see that this was to be the way of the air force in peacetime and I'd best get used to it. In contrast to my previous venture into training where we were responsible for passing on combat know-how as we best saw fit, there now existed a syllabus of training. As part of the new process I was to be formally trained as a qualified flying instructor (QFI) and for this task I was placed into the hands of a fellow Scot, and first class instructor, Flight Lieutenant Steadman.

Steadman had previously been posted to the United States where he had served as an instructor under the American system. He was now awaiting demobilisation and was looking forward to returning 'Stateside' where his wife and family had established their home. In the interim he was tasked with making an instructor of me and he did so admirably. He imparted a great deal of knowledge and experience, particularly in the realm of multi-engine training. The American pilots were taught the management of a 'twin' when an engine failed, whereas I had been left to my own devices with a resultant term in the Truro Infirmary.

Day after day we failed engine after engine in all modes of flight. My experience, ability and confidence grew with every sortie and I came to appreciate the errors which had led to my devastating Mosquito crash two years earlier at Predannack. I had not been alone in discovering the challenge of asymmetric flight in a Mosquito. As the result of numerous accidents, it became necessary to have one's logbook endorsed each month to the effect that single-engine flying had been practised within the preceding thirty days. I recognised the merit in such formal multi-engine training and took measures to not only acquire the manipulative skills, but to focus upon the techniques employed in imparting such knowledge. I was awarded my c-class instructor rating that September and commenced instructing on the Mosquito with 54 OTU. Newly qualified, I set about putting into practice many of the valuable lessons that the good flight lieutenant had taught me. This dedication to multi-engine training would become somewhat of a personal crusade in the ensuing years.

In April of 1947 our second daughter, Susan, was born. Shortly after, 54 OTU merged with 13 OTU to form 228 Operational Conversion Unit (OCU) where I was involved in Mosquito, and more specifically, night fighter training. Endorsements, ground controlled intercepts (GCI), air-to-air cine and target work filled my days and nights, yet interspersed between my many training hops, I also underwent training of my own. Late in 1947 I furthered my instrument flying experience on a course at Church Fenton and was later awarded a 'master green card' which, in simple terms, permitted me to nominate the weather I was able to fly in. A short time later, in March of 1948, I passed an officers advanced training course and was subsequently promoted to squadron leader. As a new squadron leader I was given my first unit to command, No. 1 Training Squadron of 228 OCU.

The promotion was in many ways due to my station commander, Group Captain Lowe. A fine officer, he had scared myself and two other would-be squadron leaders of the time into completing our promotion exams. Another commander, Group Captain Ryan, subsequently pushed to have me assessed for suitability as a permanently commissioned officer and again I was rewarded for their persistence and granted my permanency.

My time with the training units was characterised by the presence of such outstanding senior officers. Another was Wing Commander Desmond Hughes, who had been a highly decorated night fighter pilot and ultimately attained the rank of air vice-marshal. He and his wife Pamela, an artistic lady, became friends of Doreen and I. Whilst Desmond had undoubtedly cheated death on a number of occasions in combat, he was to be beset by tragedy of another kind during his time with us at RAF Leeming.

Desmond and Pamela had gone out for the afternoon and left their baby son in the care of a young nursemaid at their married quarters, only a short distance from our own. I was sitting and reading at the time when the nursemaid, crying a storm, entered our residence carrying the baby. I took the child from her and feeling he was ice cold and not breathing, I commenced CPR. Shortly the medicos arrived and took over before departing with a flurry. All of our combined efforts were to no avail and Doreen and I sat and endured a dreadful wait for Desmond and Pamela to return home.

Such was life in the post-war RAF. Rather than the wartime rarity of one's wife being nearby, RAF bases became communities. Despite a shortage of married quarters, families started to grow and activities that had been put on hold through the war years began to resurface. 'Dining-in nights', rifle shooting, air firing competitions and rugby all contributed to the tapestry of service life. Having been one of the few wives who had been at hand whilst I served actively, Doreen noted the transformation of service life at very close quarters.

Leeming was our first peacetime posting and it was a well established pre-war station with all brick buildings and no Nissen huts. There was a sense of permanency about the brick barrack blocks, chapel, sick quarters and sports fields. A patch of lovely houses built around a square served as married quarters and to our delight we were allocated one of these. About six were for squadron leaders, two larger houses for wing commanders and on the fourth side of the square an enormous house for the station commander, a group captain. There was a pre-war allocation of batmen for the married quarters so, as a squadron leader, we had to share a batman with the chap next door. In theory, the batman's duties were solely based around the care of the officer; cleaning shoes, buttons, ironing shirts and pressing uniforms, etc. In reality, the batman performed the role of a domestic servant. The winter of 1946 was the coldest on record in Yorkshire and by January 1947 the whole station was closed down as pipes were frozen and there was no heating. They left us in married quarters as we had our own rather meagre heating, in fact we moved into a very small sitting room off the kitchen which had a fireplace and was intended as the batman's room. Another feature of the station was a transit camp for German prisoners of war and these men were sent out around the married patch to work in the gardens!

The ground was frozen for about one or two feet down so no work was possible and these wretched POWs just shuffled around looking utterly miserable. Fortunately they were soon moved on and repatriated.

Mac was scouting around looking for another car for us and he found one in a sort of farmyard at the back of a favourite cafe we frequented from time to time. It was a 1932 Sunbeam, navy blue with matching real leather seats and had an all aluminium body. It had a marvellous window lever on the driver's side; just one elbow movement and the window slid down. There was also a silver vase for flowers in the middle of the dashboard and it had big, wide running boards. This wonderful old car had become a chicken house in the yard so required a lot of sorting out but we loved it. We loved the whole area of Yorkshire around Leeming and had picnics on the moors and in the dales by the wild rivers where Mac showed me how he could tickle trout. A skill learned during his boyhood days in Scotland.

It was at this time that the RAF reinstated promotion exams and incorporated a staff college entrance exam. The station commander called Mac and two other squadron leaders into his office and gave them the horrifying news that he had submitted their names and they were given an order to pass or else. After much anxious study and toil they did in fact all pass.

During our time at Leeming, battle dress came in for everyday wear which saved the "best blue" for formal wear. Also the wearing of mess kit was reinstated for dining-in nights and all the pre-war pilots, Mac included, could show off as they had mess kit as part of their pre-war dress. Mess kit consisted of knee high black patent leather boots – the original wellingtons, very tight trousers which were worn over the top with a strap under the boot and braces to tighten them up. A white dress shirt with a stiff collar, black wing tie and a short jacket with the rank stripes in gold braid on the sleeves and miniature medals were worn. It was a very attractive outfit. The batmen were expert at preparing the trousers for wear; they had to be threaded over the boots and rolled back so they could be climbed into with boot hooks to pull up the boots before rolling up the trousers.

The stores department also began issuing items to the married quarters as per pre-war lists. We received some amazing deliveries to our married quarter such as fish kettles big enough to bath a baby in and chamber pots; "Officers for the use of" with blue rims for junior officers and gold rims for senior officers. Furthermore we were issued six per house!

During the war our houses had been used to billet Canadian troops and, as a result, we found chewing gum everywhere – under lavatory seats and any handy ledges throughout the house. We found the back garden, or jungle, knee deep in empty cans just thrown out the back. We had a lovely Aga cooker in the kitchen which was a boon through the cold winter.

The national rifle shooting competition was also re-started at Bisley and all the services sent teams to the main competition. The schools competition which Mac's school took part in pre-war was held the week prior to the open competition. One of our neighbours, a wing commander, was a keen shot and coached a very good team for the Bisley meet. Mac became a member and they had great success, winning numerous medals. In addition to the formal presentations, Mac won a lot of money in sweepstakes and also qualified as one of the 'Queen's Hundred'.

Wednesdays featured sports afternoons and in the winter rugby was the game of choice. I used to wheel the pram down to the sports field to watch the game and invariably there would be an ambulance carting someone off. I would search the field for Mac who would eventually appear unscathed, though at 38 he decided that he was getting too old for rugby. Particularly for the Boxing Day match between the officers and NCOs which usually became a blood bath!

There was one very strange incident in our time at Leeming. We had a very badly scarred pilot, Dan Halifax, who had been shot down during the war and had suffered substantial burns about his face. He was undertaking a refresher course at the OCU when he unfortunately lost control of his aircraft and was killed. Dan's mother wanted his ashes scattered over the Yorkshire countryside, so I went up in an Oxford with a navigator to carry out her wishes. We had Dan's remains in a very large OHMS envelope and the idea was to open the window in the Oxford and tip the ashes out, however, what I knew but my navigator didn't was that if you opened the window a tiny bit the air was sucked out from the aircraft, but if you opened the window wide the air blew back in. So, of course, the window was flung wide open and most of Dan came flying back into the aircraft. The pilots would say that part of the ashes still remained throughout the Oxford for years to come and that Dan had clocked up more hours than most of us!

There was a strange sequel to this tale. A new WAAF on the station was walking past the sick quarters building after duty late one night and saw a tall officer with a scarred face standing alone. She hurried on past but mentioned it to friends the next day. When quizzed further, the WAAF gave a description of a pilot that fitted the late Dan Halifax.

Not long after the Desmond Hughes' family tragedy at Leeming, he was posted away and George Powell Sheddon became our new CO. In contrast to the sad departure of our former boss, Powell Sheddon was a fun and upbeat chap, characterised by a very heavy stutter. He had flown in the Battle of Britain with Douglas Bader's 242 Squadron, shot down a Dornier 17, been shot down himself and won the Distinguished Flying Cross. He had even rated a mention, complete with stutter, in Paul Brickhill's famous novel, *Reach For The Sky*:

> "To the side another Dornier was diving, trailing fire and smoke, and a voice shouted in his ears, 'F-f-f-flamer!' Powell Sheddon had scored."

As our post-war CO, George was to lead us for the Battle of Britain flypast. A much practised and choreographed display, it was an exercise in precision formation flying. The event bore special significance for us all and it was an honour to participate. When the day arrived we formed up as rehearsed and flew the designated route, executing turns on the command of our leader. Approaching a significant turning point and central to the display, we awaited the order to turn. The drama of the moment must have got to George as his stutter surfaced worse than ever at the point when he was to call, "Le-Le-Lef-Lef-Left-T-T-T-Tu…" Our turning point was sliding under the bellies of our Mosquitos, but George had stalled on the critical command. Everyone had tensed up when, "TURN!" spat through our headphones. With great relief we wheeled the formation to port; better late than never.

On another occasion, George and I were taking part in an 'escape and evade' exercise in which we were driven to the middle of nowhere and unceremoniously dropped in pairs at various places in the moors and foothills. We had no idea where we were and our only aid was a map with a 'safe refuge' clearly marked. Our task was to make it to the refuge without being observed by the police and army lads who were playing the role of our foe. On ascertaining one's location, the next step was to travel by night and rest up by day. In all the exercise took three days, our diet consisted of blackberries, turnips and stolen eggs. At some point George was captured by rather zealous police officers and taken to the nick for interrogation. On the way he ate his map; all of it! He was then taken to the top floor of the police station where he was to be questioned and in an unguarded moment made for the window and leapt out. The shocked officers took some time to react, but were able to recapture the limping wing commander as the jump to freedom had rather seriously damaged an ankle.

On the appropriate occasions, the medals were pulled from the drawer and worn over the left breast pocket but for everyday use representative rows of ribbons sufficed. As with any unit immediately following the war, there were a number of highly decorated pilots circulating through the system and these chaps would have quite a handful on display. One such squadron leader at Leeming had sewn his array of gallantry awards in a rather haphazard fashion and some of the ribbons were already starting to show signs of wear despite the passage of only a few years. George caught a glimpse of this scruffy display and fronted the officer concerned, advising him that,

"Willie, your medals are a disgrace!" The officer concerned looked down at the dishevelled, but imposing, collection and replied simply, "Yes Sir. I wasn't very brave."

My time at the training unit drew to a close in October 1948. My final assessment from Wing Commander Powell Sheddon DFC ranked my performance as a fighter pilot at the highest attainable level; 'exceptional'. I was both proud and satisfied with an assessment I had worked hard to attain. I had learnt a great deal in my time as an instructor and would never forget the invaluable lessons I had learnt in flying the Mosquito, particularly on one engine. I was keen to have the opportunity to share this knowledge and devise a structured means of maintaining the skill at squadron level. The RAF provided me with the perfect vehicle to execute my goal. For the first time I was to command my own fighter squadron.

CHAPTER FOURTEEN

At The Helm

I assumed command of 25 Squadron at RAF West Malling, Kent in November of 1948 and was again flying the now familiar, de Havilland Mosquito. As I drove the old Sunbeam through the front gate, I was very excited at the prospect of my own squadron and the years to come did not disappoint. This was to be the happiest posting of my life.

Settling into any new posting can prove challenging, let alone settling in as the new 'first time' boss. Fortunately, there was chemistry from day one and I was supported by a splendid group of people through all ranks and positions. My NCOs, officers, flight commanders, nav leaders, adjutant and 'Chiefy', to a man, were first class. All ranks of the squadron would 'parade' at a nearby pub on a regular basis and the harmony seemed to stem from there. It may also explain Flight Sergeant Basset's ultimate post-RAF career as a publican in the town of West Malling.

In the cockpit I was busy with navigation exercises, or 'cross countries', aerial gunnery, asymmetrics, asymmetrics, asymmetrics and more asymmetrics. I was now in the position to put into practice my philosophy of single-engine flight in a multi-engined aeroplane. Gleaning the best lessons from Flight Lieutenant Steadman's teachings and a formal syllabus of training, I set about instilling precision in this challenging aspect of operations. At the same time I came to know the Mosquito's strength and vulnerabilities intimately. Before commencing any single-engine exercise, I always checked the critical 'engine out' speeds at altitude as they could vary noticeably from aeroplane to aeroplane. One factor I had never bargained on previously was the effect of water on the de Havilland's wooden frame. Parked outside and exposed to the elements, a good soaking could seemingly swell the Mosquito to such a degree that the critical speeds could be swollen by more than a few knots. It was all a learning process and we all stood to benefit from the exercise.

Practice went very close to making perfect and the overall flying standard of the unit rose to a tremendous level. My personal proficiency was reaping the benefits of constant training and I also benefited from a couple of 'hops' that tend to come your way once you become a CO. One had me fly to France on a liaison sortie, whilst the other was a display of the Mosquito's prowess to the UK-based members of the United States Air Force.

The purpose of my Channel crossing on this occasion was to demonstrate the capabilities of our Mk XXXVI Mosquito, whilst also visiting numerous airfields to assess their suitability for Mossie operations. Unfortunately, I found most of the airfields to be too limiting for the Mosquito, but this did not stop the French from once again treating me to hospitality of the highest class. Back home, the display for the USAF was two days of tremendous fun. I had formulated a routine which commenced at 8,000 feet and involved feathering one propeller. Diving earthward with one operating engine, I would commence a low level pull-out and roar along the runway. Managing the Mosquito's energy, I would then pull up, invariably enter a roll and continue to spiral towards the heavens before leveling out, re-positioning and making another pass. It consistently kept our allied airmen entertained and one could not help but marvel at the performance envelope of this wooden fighter.

Shortly thereafter 25 Squadron enjoyed the company of a USAF exchange pilot, Dave Curtis. A major from Oregon, he was well versed in my training philosophy which owed much to its American roots. We had cause to visit US bases on the Continent from time to time and I made use of the trips to acquire all sorts of delicacies. Whilst Britain was still under the grip of tight rationing, the American canteens were extremely well stocked so I would take the opportunity to bring all manner of treats home to Doreen and the girls. Dave and I became great friends through this time and used to indulge in some after hours fun. As it was, Dave owned a huge tank of an American car and when flying had ceased for the day we would make high speed runs down the longest runway at RAF West

Malling. It was rather exciting, even to an 'old' fighter pilot.

Back at work, we were in somewhat of a competition with our sister squadrons, numbers 29 and 85, and had the opportunity to put our skills to the test in the armament camp at RAF Acklington in April 1949. The live firing competition drew squadrons from throughout fighter command to come and show their proficiency in all manner of aerial gunnery. The competition was fierce and the equipment varied across the squadrons. Our twin-engined Mosquitos with old-style gunsights were pitted against the latest marque Spitfires, complete with a semi computer-assisted sight. Even so, our performance at Acklington was tremendous with the chaps leaving all comers in their wake. Our squadron registered the highest score in fighter command and I was fortunate enough to produce the highest individual tally. At the ultimate level of competition with our peers, 25 Squadron had been victorious and it was a very proud commanding officer that made his way back to West Malling.

Given our success, one would assume that it was a fair endorsement of our training regime at the squadron. Unfortunately, it was seen a little differently by one section of command who didn't agree with my passion for asymmetrics. Since my time at OTU, I had always taught single-engine flying by fully feathering, or stopping, one propeller. My squadron and I would explore all phases of flight, including landing, with one prop sitting idly and its blades edge-on to the airflow. This is how the aircraft should be flown in an emergency and that is how I believed we should instruct. The alternative was to allow the 'failed' engine to tick over, or windmill, and this produced a totally unrealistic set of forces acting upon the aircraft for the pilot to counter. Furthermore, the windmilling prop produced a high degree of drag, or resistance, which led to severely degraded performance.

To my horror, I discovered that 11 Group, of which 25 Squadron was a part, stated that the *windmilling* prop was to be used for all single-engine flying. I was aghast! About the time that I discovered that this was the procedure, the air officer commanding (AOC) of 11 Group discovered that I had been responsible for my squadron employing a totally contradictory technique. A technique that I knew they were using at 13 Group. Nevertheless, the AOC 11 Group hauled me up in front of him and administered a severe dig, or official admonishment, for breaking their flying instructions. I stood there through the tirade, silently seething, but taking the dressing down without comment. Fortunately, someone in 11 Group Command must have pleaded my case, for new flying instructions were issued aligning our procedures of those with 13 Group. In future, single-engine flying was to be conducted with the failed engine *feathered*. Thank heavens!

As with my previous posting, the two station commanders in my time at West Malling contributed a great deal to the level of success and enjoyment. In the first instance the command was held by Group Captain Worrall DFC and later Group Captain Ramsbottom-Isherwood DFC AFC. Both gentlemen were marvellous people who led by example and had served in the Battle of Britain. 'Isher', as he was known, charmed everyone he came in contact with and became a personal friend of Doreen and myself. A New Zealander by birth, he had led a wing of Hurricanes to Russia during the war and in addition to awards from the Sovereign, he had received the Order of Lenin from his allies. In their time in Russia, Isher's men accumulated quite a sum of money that was paid by their hosts in reward for actions against the enemy. On his return to Britain, Isher donated the entire, and sizeable, amount to the RAF benevolent fund. Such was his way. Unfortunately, this first-class chap and fighter pilot was to be stalked by tragedy. Isher also served as the sector commander in our area and would commute to RAF Felixstowe in a Gloster Meteor, the RAF's first jet fighter. Returning from Felixstowe in the foulest of weather his luck ran out just short of West Malling when he impacted the earth at high speed.

In the wake of the accident, his widow suffered a terrible time when she was caught up in the bureaucratic process and denied any assistance from the RAF benevolent fund; the very fund to which Isher had generously contributed. The mess became rather high profile and adorned a number of newspapers with the money finally being awarded. Even so, at such a time of grief, the episode was highly unnecessary. Personally, Isher's loss was a blow for Doreen and I in what was otherwise a very happy time for us. Unlike Leeming, we lived off base as a family and, once again, Doreen did a magnificent job of getting us all established.

This was a really exciting posting for Mac, to be CO

of his first fighter squadron, and to be flying
Mosquitos too! We loaded up our old Sunbeam in
Leeming with Jane about five and Susan twelve
months and made the very long drive down to West
Malling. We found accommodation at a sort of
residential club called Moat Farm in Wrotham, not
too far from the airfield. In the bar one night Mac
was chatting to a man about finding somewhere to
live and the man said he owned a house nearby
which he was eventually going to sell but which we
could rent in the meantime – wonderful news – it
turned out to be a fabulous place set on Wrotham
Hill in eight acres of beechwood and we were very
happy there. Susan soon learned to walk by falling
down the double staircase we had. The Bryant-
Fenns, from Mac's days at 264 Squadron, came and
shared the house with us as Fenners was stationed at
the air ministry. Eventually our landlord, Mr Brown,
informed us that he would be selling the house
(called 'Greenhillwood'). We put off prospective
buyers for as long as we could then the house was
put up for auction and was sold.

We were then scratching around for another
place and someone gave us a telephone number of a
retired admiral with a huge house who had a flat to
let. We rang this number but must have misdialled
or had the wrong number because the person who
answered the phone said it was the doctor's house.
When we asked if they had a flat to let they said
that they were only thinking about it and hadn't
actually decided to yet, but we were welcome to
come and see them. We made an appointment and
were very nervous, thinking of a village doctor as
being stuffy, so we dressed in our country tweeds
and parked the old Sunbeam up the road, well away
from the house which was a beautiful old Georgian
mansion in the middle of the village of Watering-
bury. The door was opened by a gorgeous,
beautifully dressed lady, who invited us in and
offered us drinks and said she couldn't understand
how we got the information about the flat,
however, luckily for us they had decided to rent out

part of their enormous house after reorganising it. Shortly after our arrival the door opened and a small man poked his nose in and said he'd be back shortly. This, it seems, was the doctor and his surgery was at the back of the house. The dreaded question was asked, "Do you have any children?" With truth the only option, we replied in the affirmative. To our amazed relief they said, "Good. We want someone with children!" They then showed us the beautiful garden and the swimming pool – imagine, in the heart of Kent – a full size pool; unheard of in those days. So we moved in soon after and didn't have to hide the car, they thought it was wonderful. Our association with Doctor Severne and his family was so good, they became like our own family. They had two Austrian live-in maids, a mother and daughter, so we had permanent baby sitters.

Mac loved his squadron and was a very popular CO. He bought a small folding motorbike, the sort the paratroopers used, called a Corgi. He could carry it in the Mosquito, which was very handy, as he could be mobile as soon as he landed when there wasn't a staff car. However, the Corgi also served a purpose at home.

The house was on the edge of the hop fields and at the end of the summer the hop pickers from the East End of London used to come down for their summer holidays, entire families, and they lived in huts round the hop fields and picked hops during the day and had fun round campfires at night. The doctor's patient list doubled at this time and as he had his own dispensary and employed a full-time pharmacist the medications had to be delivered to the hop fields and Mac used to help out delivering on his Corgi.

The Severnes seemed happy that their new tenant was serving in the RAF as they had military connections of their own. The older son, John, was at the RAF College at Cranwell and the doctor, Toby, had been in the Royal Flying Corps in World War One. Their second son, Dick, was awaiting his call up for the army as conscription was still in force. I had the opportunity to take John for a flight in a Mosquito one afternoon and it was a great pleasure for both of us. Little did I know that this junior officer would rise to the rank of air vice-marshal and be knighted by Her Majesty!

1949 seemed to be disappearing at a great rate of knots, primarily due to the interesting and varied duties my posting entailed. In August I received word that I was to lead all of the Mosquitos in Fighter Command for the Battle of Britain flypast over Buckingham Palace. It was a tremendous honour to be chosen and I was intent on the formation putting in a faultless performance. We rehearsed and had our part down precisely, with turns and timing right on the numbers. When September 15th arrived, Doreen joined the crowds on the ground and I set off with my navigator from West Malling. Quite literally, we formed up like a swarm of Mosquitos at the rendezvous point and set course in not quite ideal weather. Patches of low cloud and a hazy overcast filled the sky, but neither was to spoil the day; or so I thought. My first inkling of a problem was my navigator's growing restlessness followed by his rather delayed provision of headings to fly. On enquiring as to his welfare, he all but snapped. He obviously felt the pressure of being the leader's navigator, but what followed was unprecedented and uncalled for. He began ranting about the impossibility of navigating with the patches of low cloud obscuring his view and asking how he was expected to track our position under these miserable circumstances. I couldn't help but think of the 'miserable circumstances' we had flown in on numerous occasions during the war, but thought better of expressing the sentiment. All the while attempting to fly the Mossie smoothly so that my counterparts could formate, I attempted to placate my disgruntled crewman but it was to no avail. Shortly thereafter he threw his charts down and his hands up.

I gathered up the relevant map with the course marked out and attempted to recognise a feature, any feature, on the ground. I fixed our position and we were indeed on track and on time. I pinned the chart between my hand and the control column and now added navigator to the role of pilot and formation leader. I would have given my right arm, if it wasn't otherwise occupied, for Ken Lusty or Bernard Cannon to be sitting in the nav's seat.

Beneath the cloud cover, the run into Buckingham Palace

was clear and from my standpoint the assembled masses merged to create a sea of humanity. Tucked in and tight, our Mosquitos roared overhead on this most significant of British anniversaries. Wave after wave of Royal Air Force machinery filled the sky in tribute to those who had served and neither weather nor petulant nav could detract from this day in any manner.

CHAPTER FIFTEEN

Green Endorsements, Gongs and Glosters

If I'd stopped to review my first year as a CO it would have been hard to imagine it being any more rewarding. I had settled into the role without too much ado and the highlights far outweighed the drawbacks. As a family we were settled nearby and it was with a very positive outlook that we greeted 1950. All in all, life was good.

From my enlistment in 1939 I had seen the development of military aviation at a very rapid pace. The war had evolved the fighter far beyond a simple biplane where oil and spent shells filled the airflow as it rushed by the pilot's goggled face. It was now a machine capable of ever increasing speed, accuracy and lethality. As the war had drawn to a close, even propellers had threatened to become obsolete as a new dawn of aviation broke the horizon. Sir Frank Whittle had made the jet engine a reality and its baptism of fire for the RAF in World War Two came in the form of the Gloster Meteor. As with its German jet counterpart, the Meteor had entered service in 1944 and was too late to impact upon the war in any major way. However, its higher speed did allow it to have some success against the V-1 flying bombs that were beginning to rain upon London. The total number it destroyed was only a small proportion of those launched; nevertheless, it served a worthwhile purpose on the propaganda front.

Now there was an opportunity for an old piston pilot to see what the fuss was about. With limited availability of a Mk 7 Meteor at West Malling, I organised to be checked out in the two-seat trainer version of Britain's first jet fighter and on a typically English March morning I slid back the greenhouse canopy of the Gloster jet. The cockpit itself had the standard cramped feel to it and an instrument panel that had changed little in its layout from the Hurricane. The 'standard six' dials were centrally located and a collection of others squeezed in wherever space permitted. No thought of logic or ergonomics here, just a frenzied array of instruments conveying all manner of information. There were other new concepts to grasp as well; pressurisation, dive-brakes and, of course, the two Derwent jet engines sitting out on the wings.

With the checks completed we set about getting the motors in motion. There was not an ever faster spinning disc of propeller blades to be seen, merely an ever intensifying whine that modulated into the smoothest of whistles as the jets roared into life. Whilst the noise levels inside the cockpit were very acceptable, the grasping of ears by ground crew suggested that this was not the case on the tarmac. Gone were the telltale shudders and puffs of smoke from a long line of exhaust stacks, in fact, the whole aircraft seemed decidedly smooth under power from the spinning turbines. Moving off, I immediately recalled the joys of nosewheel steering and the tremendous forward visibility that goes hand in hand. The Boston and Havoc had been my only previous exposure to this under-carriage layout, but its simplicity and safety of operation flagged it as the way of the future. Approaching runway's end the temperatures were all in the green and ready to go, even on this coolest of days. This minimal warm up time was to prove another benefit of the new breed over its forefathers.

Lined up and given the OK from the seat behind, I smoothly advanced the throttles with my left hand. The sinking into the seat was almost immediate and increased at a rate I had not experienced before. The acceleration was impressive as we roared along West Malling's main runway, gobbling up valuable feet of runway at an incredible rate. Slowly, with limited coaxing, the nose lifted off and we soared away at a striking rate of climb, all the while going faster and faster. The phrase 'homesick angel' comes to mind as quite an apt description of the Meteor's performance. We wheeled about the sky with unparalleled energy as I came to terms with the handling of the twin jet and its surprising rate of roll. Whilst it was not the pure joy one experienced in the Mosquito, it was very hard not to be impressed. I performed a series of aerobatic manoeuvres one after the other as the thirsty Derwents gulped down the fuel at an exorbitant rate. I then set about re-entering the circuit area and familiarising myself with the aircraft's handling close to the ground and with everything hanging out. With prudent use of the dive-brakes, slowing down the Meteor was not much of an issue and to a tail-wheel pilot, the landing was incredibly bland. No loss of forward vision, no struggle to attain the perfect three-pointer; just fly down and land. Simplicity in itself, though once again we consumed much of the runway.

The single circuit check ride before being set loose did not apply when being endorsed on your first jet type in peacetime. We had been aloft for the best part of an hour and I needed to fly a few more circuits and bumps before going solo. As luck would have it, I was not able to co-ordinate my duties as CO with the T7's availability for another three months. Finally, a window of opportunity opened and I was through it quicker than you could imagine. I whipped around the circuit area for a few laps, looking at some variations on the standard approach before bringing the aircraft to a halt. Just as my instructor had done in 1939, he climbed out and told me to take her up on my own, only this time there was a tap on the cockpit glass rather than a pat on the shoulder. And so I entered the jet age. It was a little late arriving for me, but my first solo ride in aviation's future was no less exhilarating. It was now June and I'd had my first taste of jet flying, yet the summer of 1950 was to yield even more memories that would last a lifetime.

Despite receiving my severe dig the previous year, I had never swayed from my course on training my pilots in the ways of asymmetrics. It had borne fruit in the squadron's tremendous standard of flying and filtered through to the trophy winning performance at Acklington. My perseverance in this matter bordered on a crusade and had begun to spread across the group. I had not made it my quest for personal recognition, far from it, I had sought to instill in others the principles that I was not equipped with when I was nearly killed in the Mosquito at Predannack. I had goofed up and nearly paid for it with my life and I had no intention of seeing any young pilot repeat my mistakes. As such, it came as a total surprise when I was awarded the Air Force Cross. Congratulations arrived from all quarters; Sir Basil Embry, various AOCs, old RAF comrades, family and friends alike. Personally, the AFC meant a great deal for I felt that it once and for all nullified the admonishment I had received at the hands of the AOC of 11 Group for my philosophy on single-engine training.

The presentation of the award was arranged to take place at Buckingham Palace. Unfortunately, King George VI's ailing health was to intervene and I received a letter from the King explaining that illness would prevent him making the presentation. Not much over a year later, His Majesty would die in his sleep at the age of fifty-six.

Shortly after the announcement of my Air Force Cross we were joined at 25 Squadron by Flight Lieutenant Dennis Leet. Dennis had been a student of mine at RAF Leeming where I had trained him on the Mosquito and, needless to say, subjected him to the full extent of my training doctrine. This particular July morning Dennis was tasked with undertaking a meteorological sortie, or 'met flight'. In essence, this consisted of flying the Mosquito to the upper limits of its operating altitude and taking a series of readings at 500 feet intervals enroute. It was a standard duty which was shared with two other squadrons on the base and today fell upon the broad shoulders of 25 Squadron.

For my part, I was tasked to attend the officers mess with one of my flight commanders, Cameron Cox. Just as well I thought, as it was a miserable day outside with low overcast and drizzling rain. To this uninviting backdrop Cox and I attended to a pre-lunch drink, undoubtedly accompanied by conversation relating to numerous operational issues. We were just settled when news came through that the routine met flight was in difficulty. Dennis had finally levelled out on top of the weather at around 30,000 feet when an engine had failed, leaving him staggering at altitude on one good engine. This was a challenging exercise to say the least as Dennis was looking at a prolonged descent through foul weather on one engine. I had no sooner started contemplating the ramifications of his predicament when a further dispatch came through with dire consequences. Dennis' port engine had failed and with it the vacuum pump that provided the air source to many of his flight instruments. This alone was not cause for alarm as the starboard engine's vacuum pump should have risen to the task, but for some reason it was not providing the required suction and Dennis was now stranded above the weather on one engine, virtually without instruments and low on options. Clear of cloud he could remain orientated with the visual horizon, but in cloud he would lose this reference and with it the ability to remain upright. In these most difficult of circumstances, bailing out was looming as the only alternative for the crew.

I decided at that moment to take off and attempt to lead the crippled Mosquito home. Cox objected and said that as flight commander it was his responsibility and that he should go, I countered that Dennis had been my student at Leeming and I didn't have time to argue. I grabbed my navigator, Flight Lieutenant Phil Read, and we scrambled ourselves with all the haste we could muster, bringing our Mk XXXVI Mosquito to life without delay. We roared away and punched into the low overcast at only 200 feet and bore our way through the weather with every ounce of power the Rolls-Royce engines would afford me. Airborne, we established contact with the ground based radar station that subsequently gave me vectors towards the distressed aircraft and further updated me of his progress. The situation had deteriorated as the crew was now no longer able to maintain altitude. Aware of my impending arrival, they had commenced a reluctant descent at the slowest of rates in an attempt to remain in clear air. Time had now also entered the equation as a critical factor.

On and on, the cloud seemed endless. We were climbing as fast as we could with the throttles to the wall, steering the headings we were being fed. I have lost count of how many times I have flown interceptions on other aircraft in training and in war, but today I was desperate that the system work without fault. A bit over 20,000 feet and there seemed to be a lighter glow about the gloom. Were we getting close to the cloud tops? Lighter and lighter and then a distinct break and a glimpse of blue. Nearly there. Through 25,000 feet we burst into the eye-numbing brilliance of daylight to catch a glimpse of the stricken Mosquito about to enter the cloud tops. The intercept had been absolutely perfect.

I wheeled around towards the other aircraft without delay as it was critical to catch him before he descended into the main body of cloud. Throttling back so as not to overshoot, I edged alongside our squadron mates. I spoke to Dennis and laid out our plan; hastily conceived, but a plan nonetheless. He still had a vertical speed indicator (VSI) available and could thereby set a slow rate of descent in company with a constant power setting. I had him establish this descent and then pulled ahead and to his right, so that he was effectively in the formation position of left echelon to me. Formed up, nice and tight, I had just established the lead when we descended back into the cloud. Somewhat settled in this unorthodox descent, I contacted the GCI station and called for vectors that would lead us over the Channel, just off RAF Manston. My thinking revolved around the fact that Manston was equipped with a huge runway and was built during World War Two to offer damaged aircraft limping home from Europe a readily available and non-limiting landing field.

The trip down was far slower and a little more tense than our high speed ascent, but it was proving controlled and effective. As we reached the lower levels my navigator took over control of the descent and approach to Manston using his on-board equipment. He provided a beautifully smooth run down the hill and steered me towards the beckoning runway, all the while in dense cloud with Dennis tucked in on my wing. Through 1,000 feet we were in a stable descent and hopefully aligned with our final approach course. Lower, lower, lower, and still nothing. Through 500 feet, nothing but cloud. 300 feet.... Visual! Dead ahead lay the runway; my nav had put us right on the spot. We were slightly over our approach speed but with the longest runway in south-eastern England looming large it was not a problem. I told Dennis it was over to him and pulled well away to give him room. Without delay his wheels slowly lowered from their wells beneath the wings and his aircraft set for landing. His wheels had seemingly only just locked down when he was reunited with the earth, rolling out for a perfectly safe arrival with one engine out of action. I transmitted a brief message of congratulations to Dennis before powering up and continuing on back to West Malling, where I resumed my pre-lunch drink at the mess. With his aircraft now stranded at Manston, Dennis was trucked back to base and joined us in the mess some time later.

For our efforts that day both Dennis and I received a Green Endorsement in our logbooks. (Personally, I believe that my navigator, Flight Lieutenant Read, should also have received recognition for his magnificent effort.) The Green Endorsement was a very high level of commendation, though some joked that it allowed the air ministry to escape having to award me another AFC! Entered, logically enough, in green ink, the entry reads:

<u>Instances of avoidance by exceptional flying skill
and judgement of loss of, or damage to, aircraft or
personnel.</u>
*Squadron Leader McGlashan took off from RAF
West Malling in bad weather to lead another
Mosquito aircraft in difficulties into RAF Manston.
He carried out a well judged and accurate descent
through cloud and enabled the other aircraft to land
safely. I consider his initiative and coolness,
combined with a high standard of airmanship
avoided what might have been a very serious
accident.*
D.M Gordon
G.Capt Commanding 11 Group.
21 August 1950.

The Green Endorsement coincided with the end of my tenure as
CO of 25 Squadron and saw my attachment to HQ 11 Group.
I would miss my squadron; the people and the flying. It had
undoubtedly been the most enjoyable chapter of my RAF
career, unrivalled in terms of personal satisfaction. After nearly
two years at the helm, I believed that I had left the squadron in
very good shape for my successor. For me, paperwork and
administrative duties at headquarters now called. I had kept
one step ahead of a desk job ever since 1939, but finally the
mahogany bomber had caught up with me. Were my days as an
operational pilot drawing to a close, or was this just another
posting? Either way, my future would be hard pressed to rival
my time at 25 Squadron, West Malling.

CHAPTER SIXTEEN

Landlocked

In aviation circles, desks are frequently referred to as mahogany bombers. This epithet tends to reflect the extent to which one's flying will be limited and I was to be no exception. I was now a staff officer attached to 11 Group Headquarters at Uxbridge and my position was as operations officer – night fighters. This rather impressive name belied the nature of the job which was rather dull. As expected, I was waging the ferocious war of paperwork and precious little else.

My flying had all but dried up with the exception of organising a check ride in the little de Havilland Vampire. Twin-tailed and powered by a single 'Goblin' engine, it was a wonderful, sprightly little jet and tremendous fun to fly. Occasionally I was able to strap myself into one, particularly if I could claim it to be a liaison visit to one of the squadrons. Otherwise it was tedious monotony, broken only by the eventful social life I was having outside the office, albeit accommodated in a novel form of housing. As Doreen recalls:

> Dr Severne and his wife returned from a fabulous holiday in Ireland where they had towed their own caravan. This gave us an idea for accommodating our constantly moving life and we purchased two enormous caravans. One was fitted out with washing machine, sink, bathroom and lounge area while the other had space for bunk beds for the older children and a small room for our newest arrival, Sally. Our bed was stored in the wall and folded down already made up.
>
> We gained permission from 11 Group to site the vans in the grounds of a disused building and so our

accommodation was organised. I think we were pioneers in this field and became the first of many to use this solution to find a place to live. There was always a long list for married quarters which meant months of separation and inconvenience. In later years many RAF stations established their own caravan sites for this very purpose.

We could entertain up to twenty-four people at our cocktail parties. The favoured drink of the time was a Sangria mix and Kenneth would walk around the outside of the caravan with a jug, whilst our guests would hold their glasses out of the windows for a refill.

Though enjoyable, life was not all fun and games. I had been a squadron leader now for three years, primarily due to the forceful encouragement of my senior officers at Leeming. In sitting the promotional exams at that time, I had also passed my entrance exam to staff college by default and a posting to that institution loomed large. In due course the inevitable happened and I was selected to attend Staff College at Bracknell in Berkshire. It was 1952 and I was about to embark on the most frustrating episode of my RAF career, without exception.

It was a year of study in subjects which I found to be of marginal relevance and totally void of interest. In turn this knowledge was preached by a staff of predominantly pompous and totally out of touch lecturers. Paper after paper was required, including a not insignificant thesis. To a pilot who had spent the greater part of his career in an operational capacity, this was absolute tedium. If it were not for Doreen's encouragement on the home front and her assistance in putting the never ending assignments together, I can honestly say I would never have made it through. Doreen does not have fond memories of that period either.

The next posting was the most traumatic event in Kenneth's, and in fact my own life. Staff College – Bracknell. Fortunately, we were able to stay on at the caravan site at 11 Group. For Kenneth's part, he hated every moment at the college and became a totally different person for a time. Far from his usual easy going persona, he would have a few drinks at the pub and want to pick fights with one and all. It riled him in a way that combat never had and, meanwhile, I had the miserable job of typing up all of his notes. Even I could see that it was a load of useless tripe. The year wasn't a total loss though as I became pregnant with daughter number four.

As a member of No. 42 Staff Course, one was also called upon to participate in a pantomime that consisted of a number of short, supposedly humorous acts. It was another exercise in rounding the total character of senior officers at large, no doubt. Rather appropriately, the inside cover of the evening's programme featured a cartoon with two cows surveying a sign warning, "Beware of the bull!" It was yet another case of life mimicking art. For my part, I was selected to participate in a scene involving a court martial and the irony was far from lost given my present state of mind.

Even further away from the classroom we occasionally undertook field trips or attachments to broaden our horizons and provide some degree of inter-service insight. These were the most enjoyable aspect of my term at Bracknell and offered similar relief to that which schoolboys find on excursions. We investigated supply issues by visiting dockyards and ship manufacturers. Some were attached to the school of infantry where they saw the application of land-borne firepower. I tended to see more of the Royal Navy.

Firstly, I was aboard the aircraft carrier, HMS *Illustrious* for a first hand demonstration of naval aviation in an exercise dubbed 'Shopwindow'. We witnessed jets catching the wire and coming to an abrupt halt on the carrier's pitching deck, transfers of men between vessels with little more than a chair with block and tackle and submarines that drew to a very threatening distance before breaking to the surface. I'm not sure how much learning I gleaned from the exercise, but it was most enjoyable nevertheless.

Later in the year we underwent a variety of attachments both at home and abroad. I secured a spot with the Royal Navy at Portland and took to sea about the British Isles in a destroyer, whilst others were sent aboard submarines. It was a very interesting and enjoyable voyage and I had little trouble gaining my sea legs. I had even less trouble taking to the officers' preferred beverage of pink gin and the whole experience was quite social. Some of my course mates were a little less fortunate and spent a good deal of time heaving over the side railing. One officer, like me, did not have this trouble and was heard to say of his submariner comrades, "Of course, it's really quite smooth once you're thirty feet down."

Another staff college visit that caught my interest was to the Irish Coast. Here we were shown a pier in Southern Ireland that extended well out from shore and its purpose during the war, we were told, was to fuel and service German U-Boats. The issue of neutrality was raised and having served at Aldergrove in defence of the shipping routes, it was a chilling reminder of our secondary operational purpose; to destroy the Irish Air Force should they side with the Germans.

At year's end I was summoned to the commandant's office and advised that I had just scraped through. It was just a pass, but that was good enough for me. I couldn't leave quickly enough and get back to a squadron, group, or wherever they chose to send me. I didn't have long to wait and my next posting was 90 Group Headquarters at Medmenham, near Henley on Thames. Another desk job and limited flying beckoned, but at least it wasn't staff college!

90 Group HQ was a secretive signals unit and the group inherited the signals, radio and countermeasures functions of the wartime RAF. Whilst it was not a fighter command squadron, I was able to fly most weeks for an hour, or so, and usually from the airfield at White Waltham. It was barely enough hours to keep my hand in and qualify for 'flying pay', but nevertheless it was flying. I sampled a variety of aircraft from the whistling Vampires and Meteors to the piston-powered twins, Anson and Oxford. However, the highlight was always the opportunity to take a Mosquito for some re-familiarisation, though this happened all too infrequently. The flying in the jet types was more prevalent as there was a tenuous link to my current role and previous experience. As part of the 'new' RAF, units that had once been known as 'night fighters' were now being redefined as 'all weather squadrons'. This was by virtue of the evolution of radar-equipped versions of the Vampire and Meteor and afforded me the chance to occupy an ejection seat as opposed to an office chair.

My posting at 90 Group also saw me back on the rifle range at Bisley once again. I would shoot at service week amongst other meetings and enjoyed success both on and off the mound.

There was quite a bit of money to be made by entering sweeps and such things; and make it I did. This inevitably led to celebration and the drinking of beer with one's mates. 90 Group HQ was ideally suited for such fun as it was in the heart of a great pubbing area, centred about the Fox and Hound.

> 90 Group Mess and HQ were housed in a beautiful stone-built country house by the Thames. It was a totally different bunch of people from our previous postings within fighter command. The signals group folk included a lot of boffins, with whom we shared a wonderful time at the many great pubs in the area. Kenneth calmed down and became his old self again at this time. Jill was born and, shortly after, christened at the Chapel on base by the Padre, Group Captain McGlashan; the only other McGlashan in the RAF. Jill, like our other daughters, wore the robe fashioned from Kenneth's Dunkirk parachute, which had now most definitely achieved heirloom status within our family.

The year ticked over into 1953 and my next move took me to the other side of the fence for a fighter pilot; transport command. Again I was attached to headquarters, on this occasion at Upavon in Wiltshire. There was no RAF caravan site this time, so the McGlashan clan settled their mobile residence at a very acceptable civilian site in Oare.

My job was flight safety officer in what was the burgeoning field of accident investigation. The reality of wartime meant that accidents were often simply looked at as a matter of attrition. The time and manpower was not available for much more than a rudimentary enquiry into non-combat losses. In the post-war era, the RAF recognised the cost in terms of people and equipment that accidents brought about and sought to learn from others' mistakes with a view to future prevention. My predecessor, a Polish chap, had designed a system whereby incidents and accidents had been not only investigated, but recorded in a systematic manner. Stemming from this data was a swathe of statistics and very noticeable trends. He had done a fantastic job and I inherited a first-class system with which to operate. We no longer viewed accidents solely as 'pilot error' and attempted to dissect a more accurate explanation to the true cause. This was our best chance at avoiding a repeat performance by some other unfortunate crew at a later date.

It was an interesting assignment and I was ably assisted by Flight Lieutenant Pullem. Together we continued on the good work that had been started and were responsible for a number of safety initiatives. I was also able to keep my hand in doing an amount of 'communication flying'. Some of this was aerobatic in nature as I'd been checked out on the Balliol, an advanced trainer with a lone powerful piston engine up front.

For the first time in some while, my flying would actually increase over the next year, but not under the banner of transport command. The global situation had become unsettled with conflict in the Suez Canal and the RAF was responding accordingly. In turn, I was advised that I was required overseas, not in Suez, but distant nevertheless, to another headquarters unit. There were to be no stone buildings on the Thames this time, I was on my way to Nicosia, Cyprus.

CHAPTER SEVENTEEN

Cyprus, EOKA and the Golden Bowler

As it turned out, the posting to Cyprus could not have arrived at a worse time. Aside from having a young family, I had just received word from South Africa that my father had died. His estate was a complicated matter and I felt that I needed to attend to it before I could be posted anywhere. I sought to step down from the deployment and take leave to settle these issues on behalf of my family. My request fell upon deaf ears and the RAF duly denied me leave of any type, for any period and advised me that the posting was to go ahead as previously instructed. Without delay, I packed my bags and readied myself to fly to Cyprus where I would be attached to AHQ Levant, Nicosia. Doreen and the family would gather up what was needed and join me in due course.

Whilst the Suez crisis was grabbing much of the headline press, the situation in Cyprus was of a particularly nasty nature. In an awkward campaign, Cyprus was seeking its independence from the United Kingdom, which was not a unique situation in the post World War Two landscape. Unrest dated back as far as 1944 with clashes between troops and rioters. The unstable climate was heated further as more British troops were withdrawn from their bases in Egypt and moved to the small Mediterranean island where a new British Middle East HQ was established. The heightened military presence only furthered the nation's resolve for self-determination.

Behind the struggle lay EOKA, which in English stood for, the 'National Organisation of Cypriot Fighters'. They lived up in the mountains and some of the villages were their safe havens and whilst their campaign was at times referred to as guerilla warfare, the reality is that they were terrorists; pure and simple. Their cause was supported by the Greek government with funding, arms and propaganda, albeit via the back door. It was this threat that made the posting hazardous, particularly as EOKA liked killing we service people at every possible opportunity. In spite of this Doreen was on her way, after all, if you could get past the terrorists, it was a truly magnificent island.

> The RAF came and took our entire luggage, and then we went by train to Liverpool where we stayed in a hotel until boarding the *Empire Clyde*. She was a medium-sized, comfortable ship and we had very good first-class cabins and the staff was the original civilian ships crew. There were quite a few other wives and families of officers from both the army and air force. Below decks the ship was trooping large contingents of army, Kings Own Yorkshire Light Infantry and a few senior officers who were going on to Hong Kong. We were waited on hand and foot and there was even a playschool for the children. We had parties and dances in the evenings as there were enough free officers to go round. It was a lovely Mediterranean cruise on which we stopped at Malta in Valetta harbour, though we were not allowed ashore. We were green with envy at one of the air force wives who had chummed up to the ship's doctor and managed to get a trip ashore. Our next port of call was Alexandria, though again no one went ashore. At anchor and waiting, one could not help being struck by the incredible colour of the sea as it was the most beautiful deep, deep blue. Friday nights on board we were asked to go down to the troop's deck below to dance with the soldiers, who I must say were all very well behaved and nice. After two weeks at sea we finally arrived at Cyprus which possesses no deep sea port, requiring a huge lighter to take you ashore. All of our husbands were lined up waiting for us; it was so exciting.

As the 'advance party', for once I had taken up the challenge of establishing our digs. Furthermore, I had purchased a new car, a diesel Mercedes in a rich air force blue. There was a real incentive to invest in such fine automotive engineering; the price was tax-free and, for service people, exempt from duty on our return to the UK. On collecting the family from the docks we made our way to our temporary home at The Dome Hotel at Kyrenia, where we would stay until our residence at Nicosia was ready. The hotel also served as an extension of the mess at Nicosia which was overflowing with those based in Cyprus and those transiting to Suez.

Since arriving in Cyprus, one of my duties was to assist in establishing a flying safety branch, similar to the one I had operated at 90 Group. Seemingly, we no sooner had the operation up and running than it was called into action in the most dramatic of ways. On April 17th 1957, an RAF Vickers Valetta aircraft had departed from Aqaba airport, located on the Gulf of the same name, to the south of Jordan. Not long after take-off, the twin-engined transport had become a fireball in the nearby hills with a resultant total loss of life. On our arrival in Aqaba we were taken to the crash site without delay. It was as hot as hell and the climbing mercury only served to intensify the smell. Twenty-seven souls had been on board and in combination with the torn, twisted and burnt airframe, we were confronted by a particularly grizzly scene.

Our investigation would ultimately find that the left wing had separated in flight about five minutes after departure. Whilst it was impossible to positively confirm the cause of the catastrophic structural failure, we were fairly convinced that it was due to severe turbulence. The hot, convective winds and the mechanical effect of the nearby terrain would have produced a terrible combination of eddies within the air. For my part, I cast my mind back to my BOAC days within the region and recalled just how savage conditions could become.

The accident at Aqaba had further delayed our move, but finally we left the fine golden sand and azure sea of Kyrenia for the beautiful walled medieval city of Nicosia. The moat that once surrounded the town was now void of water, but filled with Jakaranda trees which thrived in the climate. The main street of Nicosia was Ledra Street but was known infamously within the service as Murder Mile. The Cypriot terrorists of EOKA had killed several servicemen, some of whom were out shopping with their wives. One of EOKA's favourite tricks was to shoot a man in the back of the neck, drop the gun into a pre-arranged passing pram and walk on. The city was often declared out of bounds to servicemen as we were such easy targets in uniform. In contrast, one area of the city was Turkish and this area was usually safe. The Turks were resisting the movement for Cyprus to join with mainland Greece and, as such, were effectively our ally.

Our favourite bar was owned and run by an Englishman, John Odgers, who looked not unlike a John Bull character. The bar was somewhat of a dive and one legend was that EOKA had thrown a grenade into the bar and John Odgers had promptly picked it up and thrown it out! Aside from the bars, there were some great cafes and wonderful kebab stalls, all just a short walk from our house. The younger girls travelled to school at the RAF station each day by bus. This particular vehicle had been modified by taking the windows out and replacing them with wire-netting to prevent any ordinance being lobbed in by a passing cyclist, a not uncommon tactic. As an added safety measure, the bus was manned by a Greek driver and a Turkish conductor, effectively offering an each-way bet. In spite of all possible precautions, a bomb was still placed under the bus on one occasion. Thankfully it was discovered before it could have the desired effect. Meanwhile, our eldest daughter, who was too old for the RAF school, went to a convent school in Nicosia and was often sent home early because armed men were running over the roof.

All officers were armed with the usual service revolver which we carried in a leg holster, but before leaving the UK I had also invested in a 9mm Beretta which I hung, concealed, from my shoulder. Unfortunately the terrorists knew of the standard issue leg holster and there had been incidents where the weapon had been snatched and used to kill its owner. Added security and a heightened sensitivity to potential ambush seemed to come with the territory. Each day I varied the route I drove to the RAF station and when we had a large party at our house, which seemed to happen frequently, we had to have an RAF police guard outside. Two chaps would turn up from the local precinct on motorbikes and station themselves outside the house with the task of patrolling around the building during the evening. Invariably they would be found in the kitchen at the end of the evening, legless, and I would have to drive them back to their barracks, leaving the motorbikes to be picked up next morning.

The British were not the only people to fall victim to EOKA's sinister ways. Anyone they perceived to be a 'collaborator' or at odds with their cause were also targeted, irrespective of nationality. In one instance, the manager of the mess was a very loyal Greek who had been with the RAF at Habbaniya in Iraq, but following its closure moved to Cyprus to be with his family. He was a wonderful chap and I gave him my old dinner suit which was still in very good condition. Unfortunately, his relationship with us was interpreted as being too friendly for EOKA's liking and he became a marked man. As such, they kidnapped him and took him to the village of his home. There they incinerated his elderly parents before his eyes as punishment.

Such was the nature of the beast. It was terribly vicious and totally at odds with the beautiful surroundings of Cyprus. There were Roman ruins, castles, monasteries and, if you wished, you could be skiing at the top of Mount Troodos one moment and an hour later swimming at one of the magnificent beaches. If you could live with the ever-present danger, it was such a beautiful place, as Doreen records:

> It was too hot in the middle of the day so everything closed down at about 1pm and we would either rest up or drive to the beach. Our favourite beach was at Kyrenia, there were several lovely beaches but we adopted one in particular called John's beach. The sand would become too hot to walk on so I made a tent which we could erect right on the water's edge, there being no tide or waves in the Mediterranean. We would then dig a big hole in the sand in which to bury the beer and keep it cool; it was paradise and no terrorists bothered us on the beach.
>
> The shops in Nicosia were very good for clothes and shoes and I bought a super Swiss sewing machine; tax free of course. There was a beautiful dress material shop owned by an Armenian called Vram who, with his wife, became great friends and would eventually come to visit with us in England. It was such a joy to go into Vram's shop. You were immediately seated and offered a Turkish coffee then when you outlined your requirements, for instance, the upcoming ball at the mess, they would bring out

all the lovely materials and drape them around you so you could see exactly what you wanted. It was lovely and such a leisurely and elegant way to shop. Kenneth decided to have a new dinner suit made using some of Vram's fine material. He was delighted with the finished product and the dinner jacket even had a slight bulge to accommodate his Beretta.

When not investigating the Valetta crash or flying as second pilot on a Pembroke in the search for a downed chopper, I was once again fairly deskbound. I managed to consolidate my jet experience by flying short hops in the Meteor, including a couple of flag-tows for 54 Squadron. There were also the occasional trips to Nairobi, Malta and Gibraltar with the boys from 70 Squadron, but generally my flying days seemed to be well and truly running down. As the Cyprus posting drew to a close, I received word that I was to be posted to transport command on my return to the UK. Doreen and I decided to make a holiday of our return trip and arranged passage via cargo ship to Marseilles, from where we would drive through Europe and on to Britain.

It was a very rough sea on the day of departure as we approached a small Italian ship named the *S.S. Pace*. Our precious car had been loaded previously and there she sat lashed to the deck, where she would see out the entire voyage at the behest of the elements. Everything on board smelled of diesel; even the food. We called at Naples where we went ashore and visited the amazing ruins of Herculaneum and enjoyed an Italian meal which didn't taste of diesel. When we had approached the Port of Naples, there wasn't a berth available so instead of just standing off to wait, our skipper took us for two slow circuits of the Isle of Capri playing loud Italian popular songs so everyone would know we were an Italian ship. Not long after leaving Naples, Doreen became very sick with stomach pains. The ship's doctor was totally useless and only speaking Italian, he indicated that he thought Doreen was constipated!

We decided to see a French doctor as soon as we made land and left the vessel at Marseilles, though with Doreen's condition we knew a driving holiday through Europe was no longer on the cards. As we left the ship we noted the captain and doctor on the bridge, waving a very relieved goodbye to us. Instead of stopping in Marseilles we drove along the coast to nearby Bandol where we had previously visited. They immediately directed us to their own doctor who diagnosed appendicitis and ordered immediate surgery. With no time to fly back to England, Doreen was admitted to a clinic in Toulon. As you could only take £25 out of the country at this time, I had to drive back into Marseilles to see the British consul for permission to access more funds for our unplanned stay.

Our European sojourn had turned into a medical emergency and on returning to Britain I took stock of the entire situation. Whilst Cyprus had been a wonderful experience, it had done very little in terms of my RAF career. I had been a substantive squadron leader for quite some time now and wondered what the service had planned for me. Rather than sit and wait, I decided to make a phone call to a chap I knew in the air ministry. One way or the other, I wanted to know what the future held for Kenneth McGlashan.

*   *   *

My chum at the air ministry came back to me in due course with the inside word on my future prospects. He relayed that the air ministry had indeed looked at me for promotion to wing commander some time back, but had decided that I was too young. They now assessed me as being too old and that was that. My air force career had stalled. Looking at the bigger picture, the RAF was posturing to scale down and I could see that it was the military equivalent of middle management that would bear the brunt of the trimming. Squadron leaders would be a threatened breed. My analysis of the situation was correct and not long after my news, the air ministry released notification of incentives for those officers opting for an early retirement. The not insubstantial sum of £7,000 was on offer and was known as the 'Golden Bowler' within the RAF. So with the writing on the wall I decided to resign from the Royal Air Force, the only life I had known since 1939; my previous occupation being that of a schoolboy.

Comfortable in my decision, Doreen and I set about organising our future, bearing in mind that we had four young daughters to care for. Finally we settled upon the idea of a village shop in the lovely hamlet of Wookey Hole. We became the local grocers and postmasters, as the nearest major post office was some distance away at Wells. Doreen would dish out stamps, pensions and postal orders whilst I would be boning an entire side of bacon and feeding it through the slicer. It was a somewhat different existence for a former fighter pilot. Things were going well so we added on a restaurant to our little concern in a section of the building that had been a bakery in its former life. This was achieved by digging out the vast old ovens and converting the space into tea rooms. RAF Lyneham was close by and many of our old air force friends would drop by and astound our villagers by rolling up their sleeves and serving them. It was a real success, so much so that we were able to holiday as a family in Spain and purchase a seaside chalet in Westward Ho! nearby in Devon. The cottage was very handy and served us well as a weekender. Our daughters enjoyed the life so much and they were joined by McGlashan Mark V, another daughter, Paula, born at the local country hospital at Wells. Once again my Dunkirk parachute-come-christening gown was brought out to welcome our newest arrival.

The only downside to our existence seemed to be the ever present English winter and in the midst of the icy season of 1964, a newspaper advertisement called for people to come to sunny Australia. Doreen and I followed up on the opportunity without delay and contacted Australia House in London. We were seemingly just what they were looking for and within a matter of weeks we had undergone medical examinations and sold up our assets. Once all was in order we boarded the *S.S. Canberra* and set out for a new life in Australia. The voyage was great fun, with the children in one cabin and Doreen and I in another. Through an old ex-RAF pilot, an Australian, I had been lined up a position with a company called Vegetable Oils. Logically enough, they were involved in the business of margarine and the like and were looking for someone to manage their transport and distribution division. On arriving in Sydney, we were met by the company who conveyed us by limousine to a wonderful old hotel, The Australia, to spend our first night in a new land.

So it came to pass that Sydney became our new home, or more specifically, Killarney Heights. I started my new job with Vegetable Oils which involved a significant amount of work as the distribution was in a mess. Up until my arrival, the delivery drivers ran the show, picking and choosing their routes and taking their time about it. I put a stop to this with a bit of old school military management. There was a degree of resistance at first and I received the nickname of 'Mac the Knife' for the way in which I pursued the drivers. In the end, they saw my way and the operation smoothed out nicely.

Away from the trials and tribulations of food distribution, we were enjoying our new homeland. We were on one of Sydney's lovely waterways when we sighted a waterfront property available in the secluded bushland of Cottage Point, right on Cowan Creek. Doreen and I decided to buy the land and the small fibro house that existed thereon which we intended to use as a weekender. We spent more and more time there and became the owners of a succession of boats; the 'Quest' being our first cruiser. I became the president of the local bushfire brigade, which could keep one quite busy in the dry, hot Australian summer. One afternoon we were out on the water when I spotted smoke rising from the direction of Cottage Point. Making best speed, we motored around to investigate the source of the fire. Rather than finding burning eucalyptus, it was our own house on fire! The heat was intense as I moored the vessel and it was far too hot to step ashore. We were too late and the property was totally engulfed by the crackling, spitting flames. In the aftermath all that remained were four concrete piers which featured prominently on the front page of the Sydney papers the next day.

Since purchasing the property the council had changed the local regulations and there was requirement to build houses further back from the water. I managed to get around this problem as I was not building; I was simply *renovating* my four piers with a new house. When built, our new lodgings were even better and we spent more and more time at Cottage Point until it became our primary residence.

I still saw old friends from the RAF and each September commemorated the Battle of Britain at the Cenotaph. Nearby my workplace at Vegetable Oils was Bankstown Airport, where Arthur Kell now worked as a flight instructor. Arthur had won the DFC during World War Two having commanded numerous missions on Lancasters. We had already become good friends in our time in Cyprus and it was tremendous to renew our friendship. Unfortunately Arthur was lost when the de Havilland Chipmunk he was flying flew into the ground on a training flight. At the inquest the culprit was found to be a two shilling piece that had lodged at the base of the control stick, jamming it from full and free travel.

By now it was the late 1970s and Doreen was in high demand organising all types of conventions all over the world. A major project called for her to be posted in New York for some months and towards the end of her tenure, I flew to join her for a month's holiday. I went the long way around visiting our daughters on the way, who had spread themselves across the globe from Sydney to South Africa, Italy, London and, it seemed, all stops in between. Following the New York adventure and the subsequent trip home, Doreen and I found ourselves wondering why we were living in Australia when our daughters were so far away. Our answer was to move back to England in 1978.

Here we enjoyed rural life in Black Torrington, Devon where we had purchased a couple of cottages and promptly melded them into our residence. I would make Riesling from grape concentrate I ordered in from Italy and tend to all animals great and small. Ian Cosby, another Battle of Britain pilot, now lived quite appropriately at Biggin Hill and used to visit us in Devon. Ian was an expert wood-turner and trained me in his craft over a period of time. Working with wood soon became a tremendous interest and outlet for me. I would continue to make and revitalise furniture over the many years that followed. Despite this wonderful and balanced lifestyle, there was still no respite from the winter. One year we chose to 'take shelter' with our daughter Sally in South Africa and then visit Jill and Paula in the warmer climes of Australia.

In time, the wheel turned the full circle and we moved back to Australia and settled at Collaroy Plateau. As it turned out, Sydney rather than Devon proved to be more central to our daughters. We had now shifted continents for the final time and were contentedly surrounded by loved ones and sunshine alike. Once again Australia was to be home for the McGlashan clan, which now included eight grandchildren.

CHAPTER EIGHTEEN

Phoenix Rising

If one were to quantify the expression 'a world away' for a native of Glasgow, the passage of fifty years and a home in the Antipodes must go very close to qualifying. There were reunions, associations, ceremonies and even the occasional autograph request, but in reality Dunkirk and the years of war that followed for me were a long time passed. When 1988 dawned I had been retired for a number of years, though I still indulged my passion of woodworking and granting tired furniture a new lease of life. It was the year of Australia's bicentenary and around my desk hung squadron crests, whilst to one side a small brass Hurricane stood on its stand. Photos of the mounts of my earlier days were complemented by my trophy from the Air Firing Competition at Acklington in 1949. They were mementos of a different time and indeed a different world.

It was the return address that first grabbed my attention; it was the Tangmere Military Aviation Museum. My curiosity was elevated; Tangmere had been my base during Operation Jubilee and the eventful raid on Dieppe. I proceeded to perform the perfunctory flip-flopping of the envelope in search of further external clues without avail. Freeing the contents with a rip, I unfolded the letter with total mystery still hanging about my head as I began to read on. The words were polite, enquiring and even a little excited; it was quite unlike any correspondence I had ever previously received. The sentences did not leap off the page, but they were definitely making an effort to as I started to get my head around what the author was trying to tell me. Slowly, the meaning of his words registered, though the significance was yet to impact. It seemed impossible, yet the facts confronted me. I raised my eyes from the page and looked at Doreen. "They've found my Hurricane at Dunkirk."

'Taken aback' doesn't quite capture the moment. My recollection of May 31st 1940 had faded somewhat with the passage of time, but this revelation brought it flooding back fuller than ever. Nearly half a century had elapsed since that fateful day in the skies over the French coast and now Hawker Hurricane Mk I, P2902, 'R for Robert', had decided it was time to surface once more. But how? I had landed the fighter right on the tidal line with the water lapping at its wingtip. When Ginge Mowat and I had flown past her forty-eight hours later on an offensive patrol she was already sinking into the fine French sand and half covered by water. How could anything have survived such a burial? How was it found? Questions replaced dismay and all I had was a single page to quell my curiosity.

The letter was from a chap by the name of Andy Saunders, who had been approached by a member of the French recovery team to assist in identifying the mystery aircraft. They had found the serial number P2902 on several panels, so the identification process was relatively straightforward. The author knew little of the salvage and less of the current location of R-DX, which left me anxious for more information. Attached was a photograph of the airframe as it looked today. The fabric had long gone, but there was the complete machine being levered from its sandy resting place, once more destined for the light of day. The correspondence was otherwise brief, closing with a volley of questions and requests; recollections, photographs, logbooks. Two simple paragraphs and a lone image had launched me back to 1940 in a way I could never have imagined.

Memories and mixed emotions had been stirred up from their slumber. Surprisingly, small details that I thought the passage of time had eroded were simply shelved, awaiting recall. As I sat at my desk and contemplated my reply, sounds and sights came flooding back. Red tracers filling my cockpit, the stinging of oil and glycol in my eyes, an inability to lock the cockpit open and recovering from temporary g-induced unconsciousness to the sight of battle-littered Dunkirk sand only feet below me. I decided that brevity was the better part of valour and kept my response to the point, with the assurance that I would follow up with a more detailed account. This was to be the beginning of a trail of correspondence between

Australia, France, Britain and St. James's Palace that would continue into the new millennium. As word of the recovery spread, so did the interest. For my part at this time, I simply wanted to know where R-DX now rested. Would I be able to see her again? In the face of a barrage of enquiries, I had quite a few questions of my own.

In time, it transpired that one of the Ghyvelde Aero Club's light aircraft had been on a training flight over the French coast in the previous year, just to the south of the Belgian border. (It was a rather hostile area in 1940, but quite scenic in the 1980s.) As the pilots had turned inland and crossed the coast, one of them had made out a shape in the sand through the shallows. The shape distinctly resembled the outline of an aircraft, though very little of it had actually broken through the sand. Arriving back at the aero club, they related the tale and curiosity evolved into action and the group of enthusiasts went to investigate. On discovering that it was indeed a World War Two fighter, the club excitedly made plans to repatriate the aircraft from its sandy lodgings. With the cost of salvage borne by the local council, the aircraft was recovered with the intention of being preserved by the local aero club. Unfortunately, after fifty years unscathed, the wings went missing the very night that they were liberated. Unbelievably, from the yard of the police station where they were being stored until morning.

Whilst all this was taking place, I was still blissfully unaware of my Hurricane's discovery. On learning of its resurrection, I wondered if the chance of a reunion existed. The 50th anniversary of the Battle of Britain was to take place in 1990 and I began to conceive the possibility of returning to England for the commemoration and crossing the Channel to once again cast my eyes over 'R for Robert'. The two events coinciding seemed to make for a tremendous trip, though I joked that Dunkirk council may well be pursuing me for overdue parking fees or littering their beach.

Fate would smile kindly upon me. Doreen and I were able to make the pilgrimage to the northern hemisphere in 1990 to reunite with the events of my youth. Interest in the tale of the Dunkirk Hurricane had spread to Australia with the Channel 9 network interviewing me about the eventful day in 1940 and the subsequent discovery of the aircraft. Indeed, the network sent a crew to France to cover the reunion first hand. So it was with public interest and personal purpose that I boarded the British Airways flight, full of anticipation though still possessing a degree of absolute disbelief.

We were met by a delegation on our arrival at Dunkirk and afforded a tremendous reception. At the helm was Monsieur Teissedou, an author and university lecturer with a passion for Shakespeare. Over the next few days Doreen and I were very flattered in receiving treatment normally reserved for VIPs, which they obviously considered us to be. We were advised that there were to be luncheons, tours and presentations, though I must confess, I was most anxious to visit our first scheduled port of call, Ghyvelde aerodrome and my long absent friend.

When I first entered the hangar I was caught off guard by the crowd in attendance. Within the confines of its walls were hundreds of people, all here to see R-DX at the generous invitation of the aero club. Escorted by local dignitaries I made my way into the midst of the throng which was congregated around the recently exhumed centre of attention. At first there was just a glimpse of non-descript metal projecting above the heads of the assembled group. Then, as I drew closer, those gathered moved aside allowing me access and the first full view of my Hawker Hurricane since 1940.

If I'd had mixed emotions on receiving the original letter informing me of R-DX's discovery, I'm not sure how I would describe my first meeting with the weathered airframe. There she sat, sans wings and skin, but otherwise seemingly complete. The indomitable Merlin engine and its tell tale V of twelve cylinders were perched out in front. Sand had infiltrated every possible space, from engine to instruments. The wooden prop had suffered at the hands of nature and two of her splintery blades jutted only inches from the hub. Remarkably, the third still boasted a near full span as if ready to challenge the airflow yet again. Despite the years, her back was straight and she emanated pride and purpose. I moved slowly, surveying the Hurricane's lines and overlaying them with my mental images of a time since passed. The camouflage, roundels and Brownings had long since disappeared, but in my mind's eye were crystal clear. She had only eight hours in the air before she was brought permanently to the ground. I reached out and touched her metal frame, much in the same manner as I may have in 1940, checking her out for the day's flying. Surreal yet so very real.

My interest was peaked as I moved along the fuselage towards the cockpit, the place where I had come so close to meeting my end. Within lay my perished tools of trade. The instrument panel, a spade grip control column and the pan seat in which I'd sat atop my now treasured parachute. Such a confined space. A time capsule within a time capsule.

Despite so much of the outer shell being absent, the frame and canopy provided the evidence of what I knew in my heart to be so very true. The port side still bore numerous wounds from the spitting cannons of the Messerschmitt. The canopy panels were shattered, metal frames were holed and the windscreen bore evidence of a lethal projectile. I drew close and leant over, attempting to align myself with the angle of the attack. Peering through one hole towards another in the glass, I could make out the trajectory as the bullet had sped across the cockpit. How it had missed me, I'll never know. This was probably the most overwhelming of the many thoughts and feelings that swirled about me. I felt like a ghost. I felt that the bullets had passed clean through me. Yet here I was. Given the fury that had been expended upon my cockpit, it defied logic that I had not met my end over the French shores.

I was drawn back into the present via some polite gesturing by my escort. It seemed that a queue had formed seeking my autograph; a rather humbling experience I must admit. I signed all and sundry, including a large artwork of my machine in full flight that someone had painstakingly painted. The crowd seemed honestly thrilled that the pilot and his aircraft were once more reunited; again, very humbling. From amongst those gathered, one of the official party indicated that he had a presentation that he wished to make on behalf of those responsible for the recovery. Accordingly, I was handed a large cylindrical object which on closer examination was the turn and bank indicator from my downed fighter. It was just as it had been found, complete with fine Dunkirk sand throughout. The glass was still intact which, given the years and the thrashing my instrument panel had received, was remarkable. So much was happening, old memories were being recalled and new ones created. I was flattered by the sincerity and generosity shown to Doreen and I.

Over the next couple of days I relived my downing from several perspectives. Most interestingly, I had the opportunity to revisit the site, not just from the ground, but from the air. We assembled once again at Ghyvelde aerodrome, which is a little airfield located just above where I came to rest and within reach of the Belgian border. Subsequent to Operation Dynamo, the Luftwaffe had used the field during its occupation though now it plays host to a variety of civil traffic pursuing aviation for the pure pleasure. From my vantage point aboard a small four-seat trainer I was afforded a tremendous view of Dunkirk and its environs. We flew to the coast and passed directly over the site from where my aircraft had been resurrected. After a couple of turns to the accompaniment of enthusiastic pointing and nodding, we rolled wings level and flew along the beach toward the location of the mole where I had boarded the paddle steamer to Margate. I stared down at the nine miles of sand that I had trudged towards the smoke plume of a burning Dunkirk. It had been the loneliest walk of my life, surrounded by debris and with a raging air battle overhead. Today it was a joyflight. No threat of attack, just a splendid glimpse of my former life and the luckiest escape imaginable.

Everywhere Doreen and I went we were greeted by smiling faces and glasses of champagne which were constantly refuelled from strategically placed trolleys. It flowed like water. On the Sunday of that memorable week, the town hall was opened for a civic reception in which we were the guests of honour. The mayor gave a tremendous speech, in French, of which Doreen grasped every word and I a fair majority. At one point he passionately stated that, "If it hadn't been for Kenneth McGlashan and the like, we would not be here today!" They were words that I never thought I would hear uttered by a Frenchman, yet they were delivered with such conviction and such sincerity that it was a pleasure to stand corrected. The ceremony culminated in the presentation of a magnificent medallion on behalf of the City of Dunkirk. On its face was featured the local hero of Dunkirk, an eighteenth century pirate to whom the mayor had drawn parallels with myself in his speech. It was all very flattering and still more champagne flowed.

Much like the event that had started the entire tale, my return to Dunkirk was now firmly etched in my memory and to be treasured. When Doreen and I returned to Australia, R-DX was destined to remain and await restoration. Whilst in the years that followed I remained occasionally updated via correspondence from Monsieur Teissedou as to the progress of the restoration, it seemed that the wheels were turning very slowly. Such an undertaking is extremely costly and there seemed to be genuine difficulty in raising the funds required.

I believe Monsieur Teissedou had invested his personal funds into the project and then subsequently underwrote an air show that was to generate both interest and income. Unfortunately, on the day of the air show it rained torrentially and the display was abandoned. The RAF contingent that had been organised was grounded across the Channel and no flying ever eventuated. Shortly thereafter we received a letter from a rather dejected Monsieur Teissedou apologising for the failure of the air show and the predicament that the restoration team now found itself. Obviously, this apology was totally unnecessary. It was a massive project and it was not for me to comment on its progress. I was still extremely grateful to have been reunited with R-DX at all. Not long after receiving the letter, Monsieur Teissedou took his own life. There was apparently infighting starting to take place amongst the restoration team and it was becoming apparent that the task was beyond the grasp of this very well intentioned group. In the end it was decided to offer the Hurricane up for sale and a deal was subsequently struck with Mr Rick Roberts in the UK.

So it was to be, having set out for France in 1940, my Hawker Hurricane was finally to return to southern England after fifty-four years. There would be neither sweeping passes across Dover's dramatic cliffs, nor three-pointers onto Hawkinge's green fields. This time the journey would be made within a shipping container, thence hauled on the back of a truck. Not so romantic, but nevertheless she will be home. As to her future, I am sure that one day she will again grace the skies. A worthy heroine resurrected quite literally from the sands of time and a fitting tribute to all who served Britain in her darkest hour.

CHAPTER NINETEEN

Looking Back

As a fighter pilot it is trained into you to have a heightened awareness of the threat lurking behind. You need to 'check your six' and failure to do so is at one's own peril. I was guilty of failing to look to my rear over Dunkirk and the outcome was not in my favour. Now, in my twilight years, I find it appropriate to take a retrospective look at my fortunate journey. In the years since the war, I have been asked for both my opinions and my recollections on numerous occasions and inherently there are recurring themes. As I review them now, maybe there'll be some answers for those who never had the opportunity to ask.

I was young. Very, very young when the war came to me in 1939. A whole nineteen years of age. Along with my comrades, I was equipped with minimum experience and subsequently thrust into the unforgiving theatre of aerial combat. With flawed, outdated battle formation tactics, it was an arena where one learnt quickly on the job, if one was given the opportunity. Our tight little V's of three made us sitting ducks for the Luftwaffe pairs that freely roamed the sky and three-abreast formation attacks against bombers were fine in theory until we discovered that bombers actually took evasive action and shot back! You listened to the chaps who had been in France and were playing the Germans at their own game. For my part, I had only a handful of sorties under my belt when I was set upon over Dunkirk and had lacked the opportunity to glean such valuable experience. However, I was fortunate and lived to tell the tale, whereas so many of my countrymen never did.

War in the air can be measured in seconds and for far too many to count, that was all that was needed. Often they were brought down by a cunning foe that they never even saw; I know I never saw my attacker until it was too late. From this assault I learned a valuable lesson and became a survivor. For me, lookout became an absolute premium and I no longer possessed a blind faith in our battle tactics. On future operations I would relentlessly scan the sky and never again be caught off guard. This was a philosophy I would continue to impart at Aldergrove and to the men enroute to combat through the various OTUs. I flew operationally from Dunkirk to D-Day and my approach held me in good stead wherever I found myself flying, day or night, fair weather or foul.

Initial training wasn't the only area where, in retrospect, we were left under-prepared. The check rides that consisted of a mere circuit before being let loose in the sky in all manner of powerful machines were also a recipe for disaster. A small set of handling notes was your theory training and one lap of the field was your practical experience. In this day and age it is hard to fathom how we got away with it as often as we did. The downside was the number of non-combat losses that occurred from silly mistakes that better training would have eradicated. It is very easy to overlook how many good men were lost away from the battle front. Training accidents, showing off, friendly fire and barrage balloons were amongst the myriad of ways a pilot's days could end without ever having seen a shot fired. The list of those I can personally recall is far too long to recount. To some I can attach names, to others, just faces and the remainder suffered the anonymity of twisted wreckage.

In such a hostile environment, where lessons must be learnt quickly, much depends on the experience and leadership that surrounds you. I was fortunate to serve under some fantastic chaps, whose wartime worth proved equally invaluable as peacetime commanders. A common thread between these men was that they were fliers. Some of our commanders preferred to remain earthbound and direct proceedings from there in a fashion that deprived them of any credibility. It also excluded them from knowing actually what was going on at the coal-face. On the other hand, those who led from the front could readily appreciate the problems and frustrations faced by the everyday squadron pilot. Many of our fine officers hailed from the far reaches of the Commonwealth and virtually without exception they were tremendous leaders. Two New Zealanders which come straight to mind are Eric Whitley and Rams-bottom-Isherwood or, more simply, 'Isher'. Both were practical men who could readily differentiate between what mattered and what was superfluous. They were neither aloof nor arrogant and listened as well as they ordered. Such men were an honour and a privilege to serve with.

The loss of comrades and friends is an inevitable by-product of being a fighter pilot. Even so, it does not make it any easier to accept. Within days of my own lucky escape at Dunkirk, 'Pengy' West and 'Irish' Treanor were dead, lost over France. Another old chum had been brought down by an intruder whilst dawdling harmlessly around the circuit at night. We lost Scotty at Dieppe and poor, poor 'Pissy' Edwards was shot at the prison fence-wire as the war drew to a close. This list goes on and on and, in fact, of my original pilot's course at Perth less than a handful were still alive by war's end. In addition to friends, there were countless faces of chaps you never got to know. It was the way things were and you had to move on. You could not let it eat at you as fear could cloud your mind with negative thoughts. You still had to fly, fight and survive.

In such an environment of loss and for all the mix of training, experience and ability, one quality that cannot be underrated by the fighter pilot is that of luck. On viewing my long lost Hurricane, the holed port side reaffirmed how close I had come to my own mortality that day. Any one of those bullets could have ended me. But they didn't. Yet escaping that German fire is only one of so many escapes that I experienced, with some more subtle than others. Within that eventful day in 1940 there was a series of close calls for me. With the Hurricane out of action and starting to smoke, my attempt to bail out was thwarted by my inability to lock the canopy open and perhaps this was a good thing. Wafting down in the midst of the Luftwaffe's front line may not have been the healthiest of moves, especially given the reports I heard later of pilots being strafed as they hung from their parachutes. Once on the ground, I escaped the bayonets of French colonial troops and the rifle fire of German infantry. Even having boarded the *Golden Eagle*, we were subjected to a Dornier's potentially lethal bombing run. This was just one day!

My next move to Aldergrove was met with some frustration on my part. 245 Squadron was to be 'relegated' to patrolling the shipping routes and hunting the Condor whilst the real war was occurring in the south-east of England. Both here and at 60 OTU I was tasked with using my combat experience to ready

others for action. Young and keen, this didn't seem to be
exactly what I had signed up for. However, the passage of time
has made the same young head a little bit wiser. Even though I
believe we would have been more use in the south-east, the
decision of 13 Group to assign 245 Squadron to Aldergrove
and my subsequent training posting quite probably saved my
life. The rate of attrition of our pilots at the height of the Battle
of Britain was phenomenal and had I been there, the law of
averages would probably have dictated that I wouldn't be here
today, having already used my nine lives at Dunkirk.

On the subject of luck, the number thirteen was a recurring
element in my good fortune, aside from 13 Group transferring
away from the heart of the Battle. I was shot down on 31/5/40,
which when added up tallies to thirteen. The serial number of
my Hurricane that day was P2902, which also results in the
same total. Not one prone to superstition, there does seem to be
something about 'lucky 13' and me.

Later in the war, the disastrous raid on Dieppe saw me
narrowly escape from a friendly 'Hurri-Bomber' raid, only to
limp home across the Channel. Near misses whilst night-
fighting and the ongoing threat of England's low cloud and foul
weather. Aircraft accidents, including a Mosquito prang that I
had no right to survive. All were instances of luck and showed
how good fortune shone down upon me. When I saw R-DX
after fifty years, I felt like a ghost as I could not grasp that I had
escaped the hail of enemy bullets. When I consider the sum of
all my close calls, I am absolutely astounded and very thankful
to have come through the war at all.

The Battle of Britain is still remembered as a turning point in
Britain's long history. To have played a part in this event is an
honour that I have never forgotten. I have always thought that
defining the battle by arbitrary dates was a little contentious
and excluded some who had played an equally significant role.
If I have a single perspective on the battle, it relates to 'The
Few', with whom I am extremely proud to be counted. By
numbers, The Few consist of about 3,000 fighter pilots who
defended the realm through the summer of 1940. Of these
about three per cent were what would be termed as 'aces', a
classification that very few RAF pilots had any time for.
Without reservation, I proudly stand to be counted amongst the
ninety-seven per cent.

For all the death and drama that surrounded us, we were

ultimately just young men. We had no real expectations of the future and lived for the moment. Be it drunken mess games or Mike Muir blasting off his Verey pistol indoors, we enjoyed every minute of life that fate granted us. When I recall the years and the men with whom I served, more often than not I laugh. It is those joyous memories of an unbridled youth that are still with me and the faces are those of smiling friends. Age shall not weary them.

Finally, throughout my many experiences in war and peace I learnt the importance of a level head. Not to get carried away with the situation, or some false sense of one's own importance. It was selflessness that saw Britain through the difficult times of war and there is much to be gleaned from that. I have been extremely fortunate to have come out the other side of my series of exploits relatively unscathed, whilst tremendous pilots and good friends have fallen. In the face of such sacrifice, my perspective on what has passed is extremely grounded. To be anything else would not pay due tribute to all who served and to those who paid the supreme sacrifice. No matter what befell me in times of conflict and the many years that I have enjoyed since, I have always believed in the importance of remaining down to earth.

The Short Tale of
'R for Robert'

In working with Ken on this book, the story of another veteran came to light. The tale of his former mount, Hawker Hurricane Mk I P2902, R-DX, or 'R for Robert'.

Now residing in southern England and undergoing restoration to full flying status, the Hurricane is in the care of its owner, Rick Roberts. The meticulous rejuvenation of the Dunkirk veteran will see it again grace British skies and when it does so, it is hard to imagine a more fitting tribute to Kenneth McGlashan.

Aside from his dedication to the physical process, Rick possesses a genuine passion for the history of the machine and the young Scot who flew her. To this end he sought to research into the background of 'R for Robert'. From these records and Kenneth's own accounts, one can piece together the story of this remarkable aeroplane.

Hawker Hurricane R-DX began its life as a product of the Gloster Aircraft Company. Built under contract number 962371/38, R-DX was one of many Hurricanes that ultimately would roll off the Gloster production lines. Sydney Camm's design employed many of the tried and tested construction techniques found on the Hawker biplanes that preceded the Hurricane's arrival.

R-DX was taken on charge at 245 Squadron on May 19th 1940. The Mark I Hurricane possessed a Merlin III engine and was capable of over 300 mph in level flight, though its range was only a little over 400 miles. The fixed pitch two-bladed prop of the prototype was now replaced with a constant speed, variable pitch, three-bladed propeller of wooden construction. Gone also were the fabric-covered wings, replaced by wings of all-metal construction. Armed with eight wing-mounted Browning .303 machine guns, R-DX also boasted the latest technology with its self-sealing fuel tank and armour plating behind the pilot. These latter two features proved critical in Kenneth McGlashan's survival when he was shot down over Dunkirk.

At the time of its demise, R-DX had the grand total of eight hours flight time to its credit. On that fateful offensive patrol of May 31st 1940, Kenneth took to the skies and set course for Dunkirk. He always lamented that his first mistake that day was not having a good look back over his shoulder. If he had, he would have seen the grey Messerschmitt 109s of JG26 of the Luftwaffe.

Despite some ambiguity in the timeline of squadron records, it is generally accepted that in the cockpit of the attacking Me109 was a sandy-haired pilot by the name of Franz Luders. At the time the German held the rank of feldwebel (Fw), the equivalent of a sergeant in RAF terms. He would ultimately go on to claim a total of five victories and become an officer, attaining the rank of oberleutnant. However, on June 21st 1941, Luders was himself shot down over England and subsequently became a prisoner of war.

Hurricane R-DX would spend the next fifty years immersed in the sands of Dunkirk before its discovery. Now, in the twenty-first century it is set to fly once more.

Postscript

On the morning of July 31st 1991, my father lost his short, sharp battle with cancer. A World War Two army commando and a Korean War fighter pilot with 201 missions to his name, he had finally met a foe that could down him: though it never got the better of him.

On the morning of July 31st 2005, I stood in the pre-natal ward of Westmead Hospital in Sydney, Australia with my two-year-old daughter. My wife Kirrily was an inpatient, carrying precariously positioned twin girls who were not due for arrival until October. There was genuine concern whether they would arrive at all.

My phone rang and the voice on the other end was one of Mac's five daughters, Jill. She told me that Kenneth had passed away that morning.

The significance of the date struck me immediately. I could almost see the two old fighter pilots, sharp-eyed and straight-backed, swapping tales in heaven's mess.

Squadron Leader Kenneth Butterworth McGlashan AFC
August 28th 1920 – July 31st 2005

INDEX

NOTES